HUMOR THAT WORKS:

501 WAYS TO USE HUMOR TO BEAT STRESS, INCREASE PRODUCTIVITY, AND HAVE FUN AT WORK

HUMOR THAT WORKS:

501 Ways to Use Humor
To Beat Stress, Increase Productivity, and Have Fun at Work

ISBN 978-0984889761

Design by Humor That Works
Cover by Lock Designs

Products from Humor That Works are available at a special discount when purchased in bulk or for fund–raising or educational use. For details, contact specialgroups@humorthatworks.com.

Humor That Works
817 2nd Ave 2nd Floor
New York, NY 10017
www.humorthatworks.com

Printed in the United States of America
First Printing November 2012
10 9 8 7 6 5 4 3 2 1 0... Liftoff!

DEDICATION

Dedicated to everyone looking to add humor to the world. Also to my mom, dad, and brothers (all of whom are among the aforementioned group).

CONTENTS

AN INTRODUCTION

Greetings and salutations. First, let me thank you for purchasing this book (or borrowing it from a friend, checking it out of the library, downloading it from the internet, or glancing at it while in an airport). Second, let you thank me for writing this book. You're welcome.

Finally, and most importantly, let you thank you for taking the time to learn about humor that works. I don't want to oversell you on this, and I'm normally a modest person (just ask my mom), but this book may change your life. Seriously.

Humor is a powerful skill, one that can enhance productivity, build relationships, boost revenue, improve health, and increase happiness. And this book is here to help you start using it immediately in a way that is efficient, effective, and fun.

Before we get started, there are three things you should know...

#1. I am not a comedian. I am an engineer.

I mention this because when people hear (or read) "humor in the workplace," they often think it means being a comedian, clown, or "extrovert-by-nature blessed with the gift of gab."

That's not true.

I'm an introvert—my Myers-Briggs personality is INTJ. I'm not the life of the party or the funniest guy in the room. (Well, depending on the room; when it comes to fellow IT folks, I usually do OK). I'm not incessantly making jokes or cracking up the entire boardroom because I'm not a comedian. I'm an engineer[1]. I find what works, I do it, and then I teach it to other people.

As it turns out, humor works in business. It works with your managers, your direct reports, your peers, and certainly with yourself. It improves communication, strengthens relationships, enhances problem-solving, increases productivity, and is, of course, fun.

---

1 While it's true that I'm an engineer first, that won't stop me from coming to your workplace and telling jokes if you want me to. Visit htww.co/joker for more info.[2]
2 Footnote within a footnote! Throughout the book I'll be including links to additional sources online, be sure to check them out. Just type the shortened URL into your browser: htww.co/example.

#2. This book is a resource.

The primary goal of this book is to provide you with a laundry list of ways to use humor in the workplace. From communication to having fun, this book covers ~~it all~~ a lot of it. Whenever you're in need of humor, flip to the section covering the topic at hand and pick a way to add levity.

But before we get to the ways, and before you start showing this book around touting how great of a resource it is, there is one very important chapter you should read that sets the stage for using humor[1]. There you'll find our definition of humor, why we think it's so darn important to use, and a few general dos and don'ts[2]. Read that chapter first, then go to whichever section or sections strikes or strike your fancy or fancies.

The ways themselves are organized by the five core skills needed to be a successful businessperson, each with 100 ways humor can help in the workplace[3]. The five skills are: communication, relationships, problem solving, productivity and strategic disengagement.

---

1 My sincere hope is that you do find it to be a great resource. If not, *poof* I've just turned this book into a marvelous paper weight, gift for an enemy, or kindling in the event of a Zombie apocalypse (see #116).

2 I struggled with "dos and don'ts" versus "do's and don't's" and ultimately decided to go with the *Chicago Manual of Style* preference, even if it does bring up memories of old *Microsoft*.

3 The mathematicians among you are stopping here, thinking, "but that's only 500 ways." That's correct, the last way is presented in the final chapter.

#3. Knowing is half the battle.

Those old G.I. Joe PSAs were spot on: knowing is *half* the battle. The other half is actually doing something with that knowledge.[1] Whether or not you actually use humor to improve your work is up to you; I can't come to your workplace and force you to do it.[2]

Let me repeat that: Every day, you choose whether to use humor to enjoy work more. It is *your* choice.

For those of you concerned your coworkers won't approve, check out the next chapter that addresses that specifically. In the meantime, also consider some of the best advice I ever received while at *P&G*:

> "It's better to beg forgiveness than to ask for permission."

I follow this advice every day with regards to using humor and never once have had to beg. In fact, it's what led me to the success I found at *P&G* and since with *Humor That Works*. Make the choice to use humor and I'm sure you'll be pleasantly surprised at the success and fun you'll find.

---

1 If G.I. Joe isn't your cup of ~~coffee~~ tea, or you have no idea what I'm talking about, Stephen Covey also shared a similar sentiment: "To know and not to do is really not to know."

2 Well actually I can, and often do, visit workplaces to give keynotes, conduct training or provide humor coaching (check out htww.co/consulting for more). The point is you have to do *something*, even if that something is call 646-543-7398 to hire me.

Andrew's Tips for Using This Book

Normally I'm not one to tell someone how to read, but as the author, I feel like I might be in a good position to help you get the most out of this particular book.

Below are the tips I follow when using this book as a resource (and yes, I personally use this every week as an invaluable tool for adding more humor to my work—I'm not only the author, I'm also a client).

1. **Reference this book early and often.** While this book can be read straight through, you can also just skip around to the sections that are most pertinent to you. When you have a specific humor need, simply head to the index to find examples relevant to your situation.
2. **Keep it nearby.** If you keep the book locked away in a drawer, you're less likely to use it. Keeping the book nearby allows you to reference it while your computer boots up, while you talk on a conference call, or while you avoid writing that email you've been dreading.
3. **Use this book as a starting point.** There's nothing forcing you to use the examples of humor exactly as written. Instead, use them to help come up with your own ideas that fit both your sense of humor and your organization. Of course, if directly "sharing and reapplying" works best for you, feel free to copy the ways verbatim.

One Last Thing...

This is primarily a business book, not a humor book. That being said… it is a business book about humor, so humor will most certainly be had.

Throughout these 292 pages, there are humorous stories, examples of wordplay, and definitely more than a few cheesy jokes—they're there intentionally to make a point or to make you smile at their terribleness[1].

If you haven't laughed and learned by the end of this thing, there's something wrong with either you or me. Either way, I'll feel bad, so if you didn't learn something new or LOL a single time, send me a message at sham@humorthatworks.com and I'll give you a refund.[2]

OK, that's enough introduction, let's do this.

---

1 For grammar lovers: I used there, their, and they're in the same sentence; hopefully "their" correct.
2 Yes I'm serious about this. Whether it is with this book or one of my speaking engagements, I only want to be paid if I actually deliver value. As of this writing, no one has ever asked for a refund.

HUMOR THAT WORKS

In order to get the greatest effect from humor, it's important that we set the stage for using humor. To do that, let's talk about three key topics:

1. The Definition of Humor
2. The Benefits of Using Humor
3. The Dos and Don'ts of Humor at Work

Once we've covered these three areas, feel free to wander off into the book, wherever your heart, mind, or fingers desire. It's like a choose-your-own-adventure book, except there are no limits to what page you choose and you're the talented, heroic, attractive protagonist.

#1 - The Definition of Humor

If you had to give a definition of the word humor, what would you say? If you're like many people in my workshops, or myself a few years ago, it's likely your definition would include words like "laughter," "funny," or "ice cream" (if you're a smarty-pants and think of the *Good Humor* man).

If you said any of those things, you're certainly not wrong, but your view of humor might be narrow. As it turns out, and as we will be using it in the context of this book, humor is more encompassing than laughter and jokes. Dictionary-wise, humor is defined as:

a comic, absurd, or incongruous quality causing amusement[1].

The definition doesn't mention anything specific about laughter or jokes. It says comic (which implies funny), and amusement (which implies fun), but doesn't outright state laughter, or jokes, or clowning, or being-that-guy-no-one-takes-seriously-because-he-always-tries-to-be-funny-but-fails.

All of those things are included in humor (except the last one), but it's also much more. Humor is anything that causes amusement—anything that "helps pass the time more pleasantly[2]."

---

1 Sources can be found on page 271. For this one, see *Definition of Humor*.
2 See *Definition of Amusement*.

Positive and Negative

While getting into the nitty-gritty details of the different types of humor is a topic for another book[1], it is important to mention that humor can be positive or negative.

Positive humor is inclusive; it is uplifting and doesn't target or attack others. It may make light of a situation or even a behavior, but it doesn't attack another person's character. It's like metaphorically walking on sunshine—positive, light, and inspiring of a song.

Negative humor is exclusive; it is destructive and targets an individual or group. It may elicit change but at the cost of attacking a person. It's like literally walking on sunshine—sometimes feels good but may cause burns.

To be fair, negative humor (e.g. sarcasm, satire) has its place[2], but that place is not at work. Positive humor is more effective at work as it includes others, builds relationships, and motivates others.

For the purpose of this book, assume all references to humor are like protons and are positive.[3]

---

1 In fact it will be a future book, check out htww.co/futurebook.
2 Negative humor such as satire can be cathartic or provide commentary, such as in *The Daily Show*.
3 Which reminds me of a classic joke: A neutron walks into a bar and asks the bartender, "How much for a drink?" The bartender replies, "For you, no charge."

#2 - The Benefits of Humor

Since you're reading this book you likely have a sense of the benefits of using humor at work. You get that humor releases stress, improves problem-solving skills, and can even help you make more money.

So then why don't you (or people like you) use humor more?

According to a survey conducted through my site[1], the top two barriers to people using humor in the workplace are:

> 1. *"I don't think my boss/peers/direct reports would approve."* (47%)
> 2. *"I don't know how."* (36%)

If you fall into category #2, congratulations! You hold in your hand a resource of 501 ways to use humor. 501! Even if you feel comfortable with only 10% of the ideas, that's still 50.1 ways you can start using humor today.

If you fall into category #1, then you're in luck because, in reality, very few people think humor is a bad thing. In fact, in a study of more than 700 CEOs, 98% of them preferred a job candidate with a sense of humor.[2]

---

1 Visit htww.co/survey to take the newest version of the survey yourself.
2 See *Humor in the Workplace*.

The problem isn't that people think humor is a *bad* thing. It's that not everyone realizes that humor is a *GREAT* thing. In today's world, it's not a nice-to-have, it's a must-have. Businesses cannot afford to be less productive, less creative and more stressful.

So, here are 10 reasons why you (yes, YOU) should use humor. And if you're ready to go but don't think your coworkers will approve, share this chapter with them. If they still don't believe you, let me know and I'll come talk some sense into them.[1]

Note:
I didn't make these benefits up. They're all backed by studies, research, and experimentation. See *Humor Benefits* in the sources at the end of this book.

Note about the Note:
If I had made one up, it would have been that humor makes you more attractive to other people.

Note about the Note about the Note:
As it turns out, I don't have to make that up. Studies have shown that "sense of humor" is often ranked in the top 3 traits people look for in a significant other and humor-use can improve your dating success[2].

---

1 No, seriously. I have a keynote speech specifically tailored for skeptical organizations. In all the times I've presented it, I've yet to have a group who didn't rate the speech as Great or Fantastic.
2 See *Laughing All the Way to the Bedroom.*

10 Benefits of Using...

1. Humor Beats Stress.
If stress is the villain, humor is the superhero. It relaxes muscles, lowers blood pressure, and improves the immune system.

2. Humor Improves Health.
10-15 minutes of hearty laughter can burn as many calories as 10-minutes on a stationary bike and may even be linked to lower risk of heart disease.

3. Humor Increases Efficiency.
Humor in the workplace has been shown to reduce absenteeism, increase company loyalty, prevent burnout, and increase productivity (all good things for an employer, but also for a rockstar employee like you).

4. Humor Develops Creativity.
Humor is highly correlated with both creativity and intelligence. A dose of humor releases serotonin in the brain which improves focus, increases objectivity, and improves overall brainpower—helping to enhance creativity and improve problem solving skills.

5. Humor Expands Learning.
Humor can improve information recall and long–term retention and can make boring material more manageable (I'm looking at you, Project Management training).

6

... Humor in the Workplace

6. Humor Improves Relationships.

Relationships are one of the most important elements of any successful organization (and of life, if you think about it). Humor develops group cohesiveness, reduces status differentials, and builds trust among people.

7. Humor Creates Opportunities.

Studies show managers who display a good sense of humor are given more opportunities than those who do not. Opportunity isn't just knocking, it's waiting around for a knock-knock joke.

8. Humor Makes Better Leaders.

People who use humor are viewed as being on top of things and being in charge and in control. Executives also believe that workers with a sense of humor do a better job.

9. Humor Can Make You More Cash.

Use of humor has been positively correlated to the size of executives' bonuses. That's right, the more humor one group of executives used, the more money they made.

10. Humor Leads to Happiness.

Humor is one of the healthiest adaptations for a happy life and is one of the best predictors of life satisfaction. So don't worry, just humor and be happy.

#3 - General Dos & Don'ts

Now that you know what humor is and why to use it, the last question is how. This book is chock-full[1] of ways you can just pick from, but it may also help to keep in mind a few general tips[2]:

DO... Be positive. Humor has the power to bond people, but can also be used to ostracize. Keep your humor positive and inclusive and you'll create a more supportive environment without excluding anyone.

DO... Use what you know. Humor works best when it's honest ("funny because it's true"), so use what you know best: yourself.

DO... Something humorous every day. Humor is incredibly versatile and can improve nearly any situation. Start enjoying work more by adding a little humor to your work every single day.

DO... Have confidence. Humor is never guaranteed to work, but one of the best ways to sell it is by being confident in your use of it.

DO... Have fun. Humor is about having fun in the workplace and, chances are, if you think something is fun, other people will think it's fun too.

---

1 Assuming "chock" equals roughly 501.
2 General here means broad, not military rank. So if you're name isn't General Dos that's OK.

In addition to things you should do, here are a few things you shouldn't do:

<u>DON'T</u>... Be Negative. Yes this is just the flip of "DO Be positive, but it's so important it bears repeating. Avoid using humor that is exclusive or that has a target; be inclusive and positive when using it in the workplace.

<u>DON'T</u>... Focus on being funny. Humor doesn't have to cause laughter—evoking a smile is also success. When in doubt, go for fun instead of funny.

<u>DON'T</u>... Overdo it. Humor is great but it can be overused. Don't overdo it and stay work–appropriate—you don't want to be seen as immature or clownish.[1] Even while using humor, retain your professionalism.

<u>DON'T</u>... Ignore your audience. Humor is subjective, so it's important to learn what works and doesn't work with different groups. Not everyone has the same sense of humor so tailor your efforts to your audience.

<u>DON'T</u>... Think you have to do it alone. You don't always have to be the source of humor, you can also share humor created by others (just be sure to give credit). Humor is so prevalent in the world it would be a waste not to leverage the great work already out there. Now if only there were a list of, I don't know, say 501 ways to use humor that you could pull from... ☺

---

1 This isn't a slight on clowns—they do incredible work (just look up Patch Adams). This is in reference to the stereotype of "clowning around like a fool."

Phew, I know that was a lot of text, but all of it's important for setting the stage for using humor in the workplace. To make sure you didn't miss anything, here are the three key takeaways from this chapter:

Key Takeaway #1

Humor is anything that causes amusement. Therefore, using humor in the workplace doesn't mean becoming a comedian or a clown; it means making the workplace a better place by adding some amusement.

Key Takeaway #2

Humor provides a wealth of benefits. From improved health to increased productivity to more happiness, humor may just very well save your life (if not medically, mentally).

Key Takeaway #3

Humor can be positive or negative. Positive is more appropriate for the workplace because it builds up instead of tears down. So be positive.

And now, without further ado, let's add some humor!

THE WAYS

SKILL #1:
COMMUNICATION

The foundation of business is communication. The ability to communicate is paramount in any company and is also one of the most natural ways to include humor at work.

At its most basic level, communication is about the exchange of thoughts, opinions or information through speech, writing or signs[1]. In fact, we're communicating right now. I'm telling you about communication and I can only assume you are nodding your head, thinking "Mhmm, he is so right about communication."

In all communication there is a sender and receiver, each with equally important roles. The sender "drops knowledge" in a way that the receiver can actually get it, and the receiver has to "pick up" what the sender is "putting down".

---

1 See *Definition of Communication.*

Communication and Football

Said differently, communication is exactly like football[1]. The sender is the quarterback, the receiver is the wide receiver, and the message is, of course, the football.

Sometimes the football is dropped, sometimes it's bobbled, and sometimes it takes 3 or 4 tries to catch it. The important thing is to keep trying until the football is properly received (a touchdown of ideas!).

To extend the football analogy further, using humor in communication is like a trick play. You can't use it all the time, but when you do, and it's executed correctly, it may be the reason you win the game (or the presentation, or sale, or conversation).

For those of you not familiar with football (or who just have no idea what I'm talking about), the point is this: humor adds spice, style, and pizazz to conversation. Most importantly, it gets people to pay attention.

As Herbert Gardner said, "Once you get people laughing, they are listening and you can tell them almost anything."[2]

---

1 If football was only about the quarterback and wide receiver. And points weren't involved. And the goal was just a saying a sentence. And if bystanders cheered for conversations. And...

2 I assume good ol' Herb said *almost* because I don't know if any amount of humor will make it easier to tell people they are a bad driver—no one ever wants to believe it.

Humor and Communication

A little bit of humor can help just about any type of communication. From adding stories to a presentation to sprinkling in a random question in a survey, humor can help keep your audience engaged and listening.

For the purposes of this book, we're going to apply humor to the most common methods of business communication, as defined below:

- **Conversation** – Communicating an idea through dialogue, in–person, on the phone, or over Instant Messaging.
- **Email** – Using electronic mail to inform or influence an individual or group of people.[1]
- **Presentations** – Attempting to inform or influence using speech, live or virtually, often with the aid of software such as PowerPoint.
- **Training** – Teaching an idea or set of ideas, through a live or pre–recorded setting, with the goal of educating the audience and building a specific set of skills.
- **Documents** – Using written documents and spreadsheets to inform, influence, or educate.

With these contexts in mind, here are 100 ways to use humor to improve communication.

---

1 Or to Reply-All to a message that by no means needs everyone to be copied on.

CONVERSATION

"I've really had to come to terms with the fact that I am now a walking and talking adult."
- CS Lewis

Conversations, viz. communicating an idea through dialogue, are integral to getting things done in the corporate world. They move projects along, build relationships, and can keep you sane in the workplace.

Using humor in conversation can be a great way to make sure people are listening to what you say. Whether it's in person, on the phone, or via technology like IM, adding a little levity to your conversation keeps your partner engaged and paying attention.[1]

---

1 After all they are paying their attention, so you might as well give them their money's worth.

1. **Have a Ball**

Toss a stress ball back and forth when talking with your coworker.

While at *P&G*, my coworker Tim and I used to do this every day.[1] We'd talk about the status of our projects while tossing a ball back and forth over the wall of our cubicles.

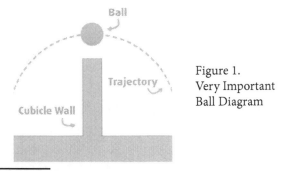

Figure 1.
Very Important
Ball Diagram

---

1 Eventually Tim changed assignments. Sadly the person who moved into his cube was not as big a fan of "Toss Update."

2. Specify the Specifics

Use very specific numbers in your conversations such as "The store will open at 9:03am" or "profits are up $32,253.48."[1]

3. Combine Cliches

Put a spin on old cliches by tweaking or combining them, like "I'm no brain scientist" or "It's not rocket surgery."

4. Steal (phrases) from Kids

If you have kids, start using some of their phrases in your work.[2]

5. Ask and Share Details

When a coworker is telling a story, ask for details to help paint the picture. If your cube mate went skiing, ask what the snow looked like. If you're recapping how your sales pitch went, mention how the room looked, sounded, and smelled.

---

1 Or you can use very broad numbers: "I worked 100 hours this week, give or take 60."
2 This is where Tina Fey got the phrase "I want to go to there" on the show *30 Rock* – it was something her daughter said.

6. Stare Them Down

Maintain eye contact with the person you're talking to, not looking away until they look away.[1]

7. Speak Slowly

Challenge yourself to speak at 50% your normal speed. Keep dropping the rate of speech until the other person notices.

8. Be Wise

While talking with someone, stroke a long, imaginary (or real if you have it) beard like a wise man in a martial arts film.

9. Mirror Language

Mirror other people's body language in meetings. See how precise you can be without getting caught.[2]

---

1 Better to do with someone you know; this can seem aggressive during an interview.
2 If you notice someone mirroring your body language (consciously or not), mess with them by slowly changing positions to see if they move to match you.

10. Mirror Yourself

Keep a mirror at your desk. Smile (or make faces) at yourself while on the phone.

Research has shown that facial expressions and mood can affect your tone of voice, an important factor when you're communicating via phone[1].

Watch out though, putting on a fake smile all day can lead to emotional exhaustion and negatively impact well-being and job satisfaction[2]. Better to find real reasons to smile: your own goofy face, a picture of your kids, friends, pets, or a (really) bad joke, such as:

"What type of stick do dogs hate? Lipstick!"

---

1 See *Smile and Put Warmth into your Phone Calls.*
2 See *The Story Behind Service with a Smile.*

11. Work with Web Cams

When talking virtually (on the phone or via VOIP), turn on your web cams when possible.

It will keep you and the other person more engaged[1], serves as a nice reminder that you work with fellow humans (not robots or disembodied voices), and it helps you communicate your message more effectively.

Research shows that in one-on-one, emotionally driven conversations, 93% of what is communicated is nonverbal (i.e. it comes from body and paralanguage)[2]. Being seen can help make sure your entire message is getting across.

---

1 I, for one, am a lot less likely to check-out of the call if I know people can see I'm slapping myself out of boredom.
2 See *Master the Silent Language*.

12. Imagine Their Doppelgänger

If you don't know what someone looks like and can't use webcams, print out a picture of a historical figure or celebrity you think they look like and talk "to" that person.[1]

13. Add a Foreign Language

Try saying hello in a different language every time you answer the phone. To get you started (phonetically)—*salam* (Arabic); *namaskar* (Bengali); *guten Tag* (German); *nee how* (Mandarin); *hola* (Spanish); *kumusta* (Tagalog); *M'ath* (Dothraki).

14. Communicate Rank

Rank your preference of communication and record it as part of your voicemail. Include "messenger pigeon" as a last resort.

15. Say It With Emoticons

For more casual conversations over Instant Messenger, use ☺☹☺♡《✎☆ in place of words.

---

[1] If you want to imagine me as you read this book, just picture the love-child of Hugh Jackman and Conan O'Brien.

16. Listen to the Last Letter

While in a conversation, play *First Letter, Last Letter*. The rules are simple: the first letter of the first word you say has to start with the last letter of the last word the other person just said.

As an example:

> Person A: "Hey, did you finish those TPS repor<u>t</u>s?"
> YOU: "<u>S</u>ure did, they're right here."
> Person A: "Great, I think you deserve a rai<u>s</u>e."
> YOU: "<u>E</u>very day is just a pleasure to work here."

Note: The other person doesn't have to know you're playing the game, though they may want to join the fun. It's also a great exercise in forcing you to listen to a person's entire sentence instead of checking out once you think you know what they are going to say.

EMAIL

"I get mail; therefore I am."
- Scott Adams

Email has consumed the corporate world. The average corporate employee sends and receives more than 100 emails per day.[1] Despite their shortcomings, emails are a valuable communication tool, bridging the gap between conversations and presentations.

Humor can make getting through email more manageable, and with consistent humor use, you can increase the likelihood people will actually read the email you send (because who wouldn't want to read the messages coming in if they were a little more fun).

---

[1] Which may or may not include all of the failed recall emails when someone sends out something they shouldn't.

17. Personalize Your Contacts

Use nicknames when adding people to your contacts list so that emails from John in accounting come in as "Numbers Lover."

18. Include a Fictional Character

Add fictional characters in the "To" field of your emails based on the subject of the message.[1]

19. Put on a Display (Name)

Change your own outgoing display name for your email address to something fun or memorable. If you're really brave, make it your very first screen name.[2]

20. Sing Your Subject

Write your subject as if it were the title of a song, such as a compliance email with the subject: "I would do anything for Sales, but I won't do that."

---

1 I was once on an email to a sales group that included "Glen Garry" and "Glen Ross."
2 This message brought to you by: skilz4ever. Yes, that was my actual screen name.

21. Activate Your Subjects

Establish a list of acronyms and codes with your coworkers to be used in subjects lines to streamline the reading and processing of email.

Here's a list of acronyms I used with a former team:

<EOM> = End of Message, for when there is no text in the email, everything is said in the subject.
<ACT> = Action Required, no date set.
<ACT 6/12 5pm> = Action Required by 5pm on 6/12.
<ACT NOW> = (Probably spam.)
<NON> = No Action Needed, email is FYI.
<CAT> = LOLcats inside (aka message is just for fun).

22. Greet Your Peers

Start an email with a unique, attention-getting salutation such as "Greetings Fellow Humans" or "To My Wise & Attractive Peers."

23. Summarize for Mobility

Include a summary / top line for people who are reading on a Blackberry or smartphone. Call it the Mobile Summary.[1]

24. Picture Yourself

The first time you're emailing someone you'll be working with for awhile, include a picture of yourself.[2]

25. Play Hangmail

Play a game of Tic Tac Toe or Hangman in emails between you and a coworker.

---

1 For for the Internet savvy you might use tl;dr = "too long; didn't read."
2 But don't use your boring work photo, use one of you doing something interesting, like the time you went skydiving or dressed up like a Power Ranger.

26. Hide a Message

Send a "hidden message" in your email using the first letter of each paragraph. Mention it at the bottom or bold each letter if you want people to know to look for it.[1]

27. Offer an Outline

Add an outline to the top of long emails. Include reading times for each section (you can calculate this based on the average reading speed of 250 words-per-minute).[2]

28. Leave with a Joke

Add a bad joke at the end of an email as a reward for reading through to the end. One of my favorites: "I changed the color of my email program to red so I can always have a rosy Outlook."

29. Anoint Yourself

Add a unique title for yourself when "signing" your name.
— Sincerely, Drew the Email Conqueror

---

1 Did you notice the first letter of each of the ways on this page? ¿Que paso, ahora?
2 I learned this from the Humor Power Newsletter: htww.co/humorpower.

30. Go Mad (Lib)

Start your next email with a work-related Mad Lib.

Here's the start of an email I sent when I was working as a customer analyst (pretend your name is Mike).

Mike—I have that update for you, but first, write down an awesome adjective, your favorite color, and a food you hate.

Dear [adjective] Mike,

I wanted to let you know how we did for the JFM quarter and I hope you've got your eye on a sweet [color] Corvette, because numbers are up, even despite the entire category taking a dive like it ate too much [food].

The good news is...

31. Brand Yourself

Create a personal logo. It can be as simple as a specific font and color, or as intense as a full-on graphic design. Use it as your email signature.

32. Improve Pronunciation

If your name is hard to pronounce, include a pronunciation key in your email signature.[1]

33. Provide a Signature Video

To really help people get to know you, include a link to a video introduction of yourself in your email signature.

34. Disclaim the Absurd

If you have to add a legal disclaimer after your email signature, add a fun detail to it to see if people are paying attention. I often use "Does not protect against extraterrestrials."

---

1 A former co-worker taught me this. He created it after far too many people messed up his name (yes I was one of them and no I haven't messed it up since).

35. Say OOOooo

Share a little about where you're going in your Out-of-Office message.

This small use of humor got more reactions than almost anything else I did while working at *P&G*. Here's what I used:

I will be out of the office starting Thursday 3/10 and returning Monday 3/14. I will have limited access to email.

On an unrelated note, isn't it cool that the acronym for "Out of Office" is OoO? It's like people are thinking "Oooooo, where'd you go while you were out of the office?"

The answer this time is: Los Angeles.

PRESENTATIONS

Michael: "We'll ask PowerPoint."
Oscar: "Michael, this is a presentation tool."
Michael: "You're a presentation tool..."
- The Office, Season 4

Presentations, defined here as when we speak to a group of people with an intention to inform or influence, are critical in the workplace for providing status updates, getting formal approvals, and influencing behavior.[1]

Research shows that audience members start to check-out of any presentation topic (even if they're interested in it) after 10 minutes[2]. One of the easiest ways to re-engage the audience is to add a little humor every 7 to 10 minutes. It makes the content more accessible, increases engagement, and is more fun for you.

1 Trainings, aka presentations for teaching a skill, start on page 41.
2 See *Brain Rules*.

36. Make a Point without PowerPoint

Don't use PowerPoint.[1]

This is by far the easiest way to set yourself apart from other presenters. That's not to say you can't display information in some form or another, just be creative about how you do it.

Here are a few suggestions:

- Draw "slides" by hand on a chalkboard or flipchart.
- Put key phrases on posters hung around the room.
- Use descriptive imagery to get the audience to visualize slides for themselves.
- Relate everything back to a physical object you use as a metaphor for your subject matter.
- Try more dynamic software like Prezi.[2]

---

1 PowerPoint isn't inherently bad, it's just very easy to use poorly. As Peter Norvig said, "PowerPoint doesn't kill meetings. People kill meetings. PowerPoint is like having a loaded AK-47 on the table."
2 Check it out at http://prezi.com.

37. Be a Stand-up Presenter

Write a set-list (a bullet-point list of topics) instead of scripting out every word you'll say. For added stand-up authenticity, set the list on a stool with a bottle of water.

38. Circle Up

Have the audience sit in a circle instead of in theater style. Present "in the round."

39. Be a Storyteller

There once was an incredibly attractive person who started their presentation with a story, and their audience listened intently and thanked them for it.

40. Back It Up

Start your presentation from the back of the audience. Walk through the audience while presenting.[1]

---

1 Yes, something as simple as this will get people to pay attention. Plus you get to feel like a beautiful bride as you walk down the aisle with everyone looking at you.

41. Remain Standing If

Learn about your audience before starting your presentation by playing "Remain Standing If..."

Here's how I introduce it:

"We're going to play a variation of the game Never Have I Ever, *except there's no drinking involved. I'll give you a set of criteria. If that criteria applies to you, you'll stay standing. If it doesn't, you'll sit down.*

For example, everyone stand up. Remain standing if you used humor at work in the last year. (Some people sit). *OK, remain standing if you used humor at work in the last 6 months. In the last month? The last week? Last day?"*

Continue to give criteria until there are only a few people standing. Then do it again. I usually do 3 sets, ending with *"Remain standing if... you've ever been skinny dipping."*

42. Embed Meaning

Be like Alfred Hitchcock and find a way to work a picture of yourself (or your kids) into every presentation.[1]

43. Picture a Better Slide

Use slides of only pictures (meaning no text). Speak to how the picture relates to your topic.

44. Lego Your Slides

Use basic animation (nothing too flashy) to build the points of your slide into to an interesting or humorous image, such as a house made out of words or a smiley face of numbers.

45. Measure with Uniqueness

Use unique units of measurements in your graphs and tables. For example, this book is 2 *Swiss Cake Rolls* long, compared to a sheet of paper, which is 2.83 rolls.[2]

---

1 Over the course of his 50+ year career, Hitchcock made 39 self-referential cameos.
2 Great, now I have a craving for *Swiss Cake Rolls*. BRB (Feel free to get a snack for yourself, too.)

46. Give a Fable Example

Share a fable to emphasize a point. Search *Google* for "Aesop's Fables" for a list of some of the most popular stories, or make one up on your own.

47. Tell a Joke

Include an intentionally silly joke in your next speech. Tie it back to the topic somehow.[1]

48. Lighten the Heavy

When delivering not-so-great news, try to find the positive in the situation and be sure to communicate it.[2]

49. Act Out

Include a short scene / skit in your next presentation that demonstrates a key point from your talk.

---

1 "How good are you at PowerPoint?" "I Excel at it."
  "Was that a Microsoft Office joke?" "Word."
2 Hat tip to Angela Mohns for the suggestion. Note: This doesn't mean you shouldn't take the matter seriously, just don't confuse "seriousness" with "somberness."

50. Demonstrate Physically

Rather than just talk about an idea, think like a science teacher and do a physical demonstration.

One well-known example of this is Steven Covey's *Big Rocks* Demonstration.[1]

Covey invites an audience member on stage, where they are presented with a jar, rocks of various sizes, and a bowl of pebbles. He puts the pebbles into the jar and then asks the audience member to get the remaining rocks in.

With all of the pebbles, the audience member is unable to fit in all of the big rocks. So they try again, this time placing the big rocks in first and, no surprise, they all fit (with a little room left over for the pebbles).

The point? If you don't schedule your most important activities (Big Rocks) first, all of the less important things (Pebbles) will prevent you from getting to them.

---

1 Words don't do it justice. Check out the demo at: htww.co/bigrocks.

51. Analogize with YouTube

If you can't create a skit yourself, use a humorous or popular video from YouTube that illustrates your point.[1]

52. Toy Around

Go to the Dollar Store before your presentation. Find a toy you can use to demonstrate a point.[2]

53. Count on the Audience

Create lists for key ideas. Have the audience yell the number out when you get to each new point.

54. Summarize to One

End your presentation with the one (and only one) thing you want the audience to walk away with. Repeat it, like, a billion or so times (or at least enough times they'll remember it).

---

1 A great example is *Leadership Lessons from Dancing Guy*: htww.co/danceleadership.
2 Like a yo-yo that demonstrates that even when things are going downward, they can be pulled back up again (and can "Rock the Baby").

TRAINING

"Training is everything... cauliflower is nothing but cabbage with a college education."
- Mark Twain

As the pace of change in the corporate world accelerates, training has become increasingly more important.[1] The ability to develop talent and build specific skills within your company will determine your organization's success.

Humor makes training awesome and learning fun. It has been shown to improve information recall and long-term retention[2], helping to make the process of building your organization more effective (and enjoyable).

---

1 Presentations, which are defined as sessions intended to inform or influence, are covered in the previous section starting on page 33.
2 See *Humor Benefits: Improves Retention*.

55. Tell Your Story

Share a personal story that relates to the subject matter. It not only starts the training on a humorous note but also lets the audience know why you're giving the training.

When I train on humor, I often tell this story:

When I was 5 years old, I never imagined I would be a speaker and author, especially not on a topic like humor in the workplace.

No, at first, I wanted to be an international soccer superstar. But, as I soon discovered, it's difficult to make it at the professional level when you're scared of the ball.

When that didn't pan out, I moved on to engineering—it suited me better. I loved math and constantly looked for ways to improve processes (including how to load a dishwasher[1]).

I graduated in the top 1% of my high school class and later Magna Cum Laude with a degree in Computer Science & Engineering from The Ohio State University...[2]

---

1 Sort the silverware when loading to save at least 20 seconds on unloading.
2 I then go on to explain how I went from CSE to humorist. To see the full story, you can hire me (or just go to htww.co/aboutthehumorist).

56. Find Preconceived Notions

Ask the audience what they think before showing them details on your slides. For example, if you're going to give the definition of a word, ask the audience if they have an idea of what it means first. This keeps the audience engaged and helps you understand any preconceived notions you may need to adjust for.

57. Explain Like I'm Five

Explain the topic as if you were describing it to a 5 year old (meaning as simple as possible)[1].

58. Be Magical

Learn a simple magic trick and use it in your training as a parallel to a key learning topic.

59. Write This Not That

Follow the style of "Do This, Not That" when communicating guidelines or rules.[2]

1 There's a whole community on *reddit* that does a great job of explaining complex topics at a 5-year-old level. Check it out at reddit.com/r/eli5.
2 I learned this from *Men's Health's* "Eat This, Not That."

60. Simon Says Play

Play Simon Says to get students to do activities or exercises related to your topic[1].

61. Equate

Come up with your own Einstein–esque equation to train a key concept, such as $E = MC^2$. Or, if x = "splish," y = "splash," and z = "taking a bath," the song "Splish Splash" is equal to x + y + z.

62. F_ll in the Bl_nks

Pass out handouts before the training that are fill in the blank style.[2] Include fun facts as part of what should be filled in.

63. Don't Tell, Do

Use an interactive exercise such as *Thumbs* to teach a key concept (and keep the audience involved and engaged)[3].

---

1 Don't know the game? Simon says, "Go to htww.co/simonsays to find out."
2 One study showed students remembered 37% more when given Guided Notes than when left to their own devices to take notes. See *Write It Down*.
3 To learn *Thumbs*, and other exercises, check out htww.co/exercises.

64. Put the New in Mnemonic

Create a mnemonic device for something you are training, such as an acronym, rhyme or sentence.

Do you know what these mnemonics represent?

- SohCahToa?[1]
- Spring Forward, Fall Back?[2]
- Cows Often Sit Down Carefully. Perhaps Their Joints Creak? Persistent Early Oiling Might Prevent Painful Rheumatism.[3]

---

1 Trigonomic functions: *Sine is Opposite over Hypotenuse, Cosine is Adjacent over Hypotenuse, Tangent is Opposite over Adjacent.*
2 Daylight Savings Time: *Adjust clocks ahead (forward) in Spring and backwards (back) in Fall.*
3 Order of geological time periods: *Cambrian, Ordovician, Silurian, Devonian, Carboniferous, Permian, Triassic, Jurassic, Cretaceous, Paleocene, Eocene, Oligocene, Miocene, Pliocene, Pleistocene, Recent*

65. Turn Bored into Board

Turn training into a board game[1]. Find a popular game and replace the board and pieces with items relevant to your training. *Monopoly* and *Life* can be good starting points.

66. Roleplay

Don't just talk about important scenarios or topics. Roleplay them with members of the audience.

67. Share What You Know

Present a tip like the old "The More You Know" commercials (you know, the ones with the shooting rainbow).[2]

68. Characterize Your Videos

If you're creating a series of videos for training, create a character to give the training. The character can be simple—just a small variation of yourself, such as speaking with an accent, will do.

---

1 Need inspiration? Check out #490.
2 Like this one: htww.co/moreyouknow.

69. Metaphor-ize

Explain your next training using an unlikely metaphor, such as why project management is like getting married[1].

70. Stand for Training

Tell people they are welcome to stand in the back or side of the room if they feel like they are starting to lose energy.

71. Give It a Second

Remind people of the brevity of breaks by phrasing them in seconds, not minutes: e.g. 300 seconds instead of 5 minutes.

72. Play Pavlov's Song

Play the same song when returning from break so people are conditioned to return to their seats when they hear it. Make it something high energy to get people excited to jump back in.

---

1 Think about it: a wedding starts with a project initiation (a proposal); you have to manage scope, cost, quality, and time; you have project sponsors (parents) and stakeholders (family and friends); and 50% of projects fail (divorce).

73. Let Questions Take Flight

Use paper airplanes to collect questions in a big training.

The process is easy. Tell everyone in your audience to:

1. Take out a sheet of paper.
2. Write down any questions (or concerns) you have.
3. Fold the paper into a paper airplane.
4. Throw the airplane somewhere in the room.
5. Pick up an airplane near you. Throw it or skip to #6.[1]
6. Pick up an airplane near you. Read the question aloud (one at a time) as if it were your own.

This not only adds an element of fun to the Q&A process, it also adds anonymity—encouraging people to be more honest with questions and concerns.

---

1 You can repeat this step as many times as your heart desires.

74. Ask Bonus Questions

On certification tests, include at least one bonus question worth extra points for answering something fun, like "What is your favorite color and why?[1]"

75. Qualify Puzzles

Include different types of questions on qualification exams, such as a crossword puzzle, word scramble, or mix–and–match.

76. Parody a Training

Make a promo for your presentation topic; parody a popular commercial running at the time and show it at the beginning of the training to get people excited.

77. Testify to Your Training

Add "endorsements" or testimonials of your training up front; include coworkers, managers and a fictional character (this one will most likely be fabricated).

---

1 Orange, because it is vibrant, unique, and a primary color of the *Cincinnati Bengals*.

78. Solicit Feedback

Ask for feedback on your training session, not just right after it's over, but 3 to 6 months afterwards as well.[1] Actually incorporate the feedback into future sessions.

Here's some feedback I've received (and my takeaways):

Feedback: *"I felt like I learned something new with everything he said. He made my brain work in ways I had never used it before. It was crazy how he made everything so easy to understand."*

Takeaway: Keep using interactive exercises to work the brain; keep them simple and build slowly to ensure understanding.

Feedback: *"To improve: Listen to examples of our real work issues and provide examples of how humor could be used to make a difference."*

Takeaway: Include time in my training for the audience to present real–life issues and give specific ways humors can help.

Feedback: *"I love the shirts you wear."*

Takeaway: Keep wearing my vibrant, solid–colored shirts.

---

1 Studies suggest people will have forgotten 78% of what they've learned after 78 days. To make sure the most important information truly stuck (the 22%), follow up again later. See *Write It Down.*

DOCUMENTS

"An author is a fool who, not content with boring those he lives with, insists on boring future generations."
- Charles de Montesqueieu

We read, create, print, and sometimes attempt to ignore corporate documents every day. They serve an important function in business as a single document can be passed through an entire company and be referenced for years or decades.[1]

Humor improves the readability of what you write and the retention of what you (or others) read. And yes, even a spreadsheet can have some humor, regardless of how serious its numbers are.

---

1 *How to Win Friends and Influence People* by Dale Carnegie was first published in 1936 and is still one of the best-selling self-help books every year. It was ranked #5 on Business Pundits' *50 Best Business Books 2012*.

79. Quote a Beginning

As a wise man once said, "Use a relevant quotation to start or end your Word document."[1]

80. Play Hide & Read

Embed special instructions in the middle of a long document (such as "If you see this, come see me for a piece of candy.")

81. Footnote Humor

If using footnotes, include a few that are for humor or point to yourself as the source.[1]

82. Shape Your Paragraphs

Have the sentences of your document create a shape (such as a triangle or rhombus).[2]

---

1 Says author, humorist and handsome man, Andrew Tarvin.
2 For example, the order of questions for #110 is intentional based on sentence length. For more impressive examples, check out htww.co/typographyart.

83. Get Poetic

> Writing a haiku
> in place of a dull sentence:
> a rainbow of words.

If you're not familiar with haikus, they are a form of Japanese poetry that includes[1]:

- Use of three lines with 17 syllables[2] (often in 5-7-5);
- Use of a kigo (a seasonal reference);
- Use of kire (punctuation that signals two juxtaposed ideas are related).

The above example contains the correct number of lines and syllables, the rainbow is a seasonal reference to spring, and the colon acts as kire.

---

1 See *Haiku in English*.
2 Technically the traditional Japanese form uses *on*, not syllables, but the English adaptation translates them to syllables.

84. Rule with Threes

Use the Rule of Threes when giving examples—try making the first two serious and the third one something unlikely.[1]

Why does this work? Comedy comes from surprising people and breaking expectations. The Rule of Threes is one of the quickest way to establish an expectation (the first two examples set a pattern), and also break it (the third breaks the pattern and causes uproarious laughter).

For example:

To the optimist, the glass is half full. To the pessimist, the glass is half empty. To the engineer, the glass is twice as big as necessary.

The first two examples set the expectation of a traditional mindset (full or empty). The third breaks it with a comment on the glass's size.

---

1 For a business-like example, review the definition of humor on page 2.

85. Add a Time (of your life) Line

If showing a series of dates, show them on a timeline. Add a fun date, such as your birthday or day when you think your favorite sports team is going to win it all[1].

86. Write Conceit-edly[2]

Use the same type of metaphors or allusions throughout an entire document (such as comparisons to the plot of various movies), and at the end ask the reader how many they were able to catch.

87. Emphasize with Color

Don't be afraid to use a little font color or bolding in documents for subheadings or key words. Limit it to only one or two styles.

88. Strike Out Humor

Use struck through words to show ~~how tech savvy you are~~ a change of thought or to make a quick joke.

---

1 Come on *Cincinnati Bengals* 2016!
2 Here we're using the conceit in terms of an extended metaphor, not being a jerk.

89. Subtitle Your Headings: Get Your Funny On

Have fun with the subtitles to your headings.

90. Make Pointed Bullets

Use a unique symbol or image for your bullet points, such as your company's logo or your initials in a box.

91. Imagine Key Points

Include small images related to the subject matter next to key points of your document.

92. Handwrite Some Design

Write portions of your document or presentation in your own handwriting.

"Write portions of your document or presentation in your own handwriting."

93. Warn the Obvious

Include obvious warnings or disclaimers on your signs.

Google has a great sense of humor and shows this in the warning message for their Incognito window (used for Private browsing such as when searching for gifts or if you don't to sign-out of someone's gmail account).

From the Google Incognito Window:

Going incognito doesn't affect the behavior of other people, servers, or software. Be wary of:

- Websites that collect or share information about you
- Internet service providers or employers that track the pages you visit
- Malicious software that tracks your keystrokes in exchange for free smileys
- Surveillance by secret agents
- People standing behind you

94. Humor the Fine Print

Include a joke in the fine print of a poster or an ad.

95. Author a Bio

Add a short bio and picture of yourself at the end of a document that is going to be circulated beyond people on your team.

96. Corner the News on Humor

Include a humor corner in the monthly newsletter or turn part of it into a "tabloid" with fake stories based on real work events.[1]

97. Encode QRs

Include a QR code in a word document that goes to more information on a website.[2] Go here —>

---

1 Hat tip to Noreen Braman, designer at *Noreen's Digital Dreams*, for the suggestion. Find out more about Noreen at www.noreensdigitaldreams.com.
2 Search "QR Code" in the app store on your smartphone to get the necessary software.

98. CAD = Create an Acronym Dictionary

Include an acronym dictionary with your document.
Include at least one fun or interesting acronym.

Here's a dictionary from one of my handouts on humor.

ASSA   The four styles of humor (Affiliative, Self-
            Enhancing, Self-Defeating, Aggressive).
MAP   The three things you need to know to create
            humor (Medium, Audience, Purpose).
ITITWEIT[1] A way to generate comedic ideas (If This Is
            True What Else Is True?).
MMM   Three things that are delicious (Milkshakes,
            Milky Ways and chocolate Milk).

---

1 Technically ITITWEIT is an initialism since it can't be pronounced as a
word. Or you could say it "eye tie tweet."

99. Announce Good Fortunes

Have custom messages printed in a fortune cookie, such as the announcement of a raise or new benefits. Distribute to employees.

100. Get Poster-ized

Parody popular types of posters to announce an idea or advertise a service. Good poster inspiration includes: movies, TV shows, or even a throwback to 90s boy band posters.

SKILL #2:
RELATIONSHIPS

When it's all said and done, business is about relationships—relationships with your managers, peers, direct reports, and, of course, customers. Humor helps you build and maintain those relationships in a positive way.

Relationships are defined as a connection, association, or involvement between concepts, objects, or people.[1] But not all relationships are created equal, and rightfully so.[2] You don't necessarily need a deep connection with a stranger you bump into once at a coffee shop, but you should develop a strong relationship with the recurring characters in your life.

Meaningful relationships require both parties (woohoo, partayyy) to be involved, and when they are, they help you achieve your goals (of success, love, and/or happiness).

---

1 See *Definition of Relationships*.
2 While the relationship you have with your computer may be important (see #313), we're going to focus on relationships between people in this section.

Relationships and *Speed*

We can learn a lot about relationships from the movie *Speed*. At the end of the movie, after the intense adventure is over, Officer Jack Traven (Keanu Reeves) and Annie Porter (Sandra Bullock) get together and, presumably, live happily ever after. They had never met before that fateful day they got on that bus, and yet fell in love by the time it was all over. Why?

Psychologists have shown that when people share emotions—positive or negative—they become closer together[1]. In *Speed*, the shared emotions between Jack and Annie are mostly negative (stress, uncertainty, fear) and extreme (they might die), but ultimately bring them closer together.

In the workplace, shared emotions with coworkers can be negative (stress, uncertainty, fear), and feel extreme (you might "literally die if you have to go to another pre-meeting about an upcoming meeting"[2]). Sadly, those negative experiences may be the only relationship–building you do with your coworkers.

But it doesn't have to be that way. The emotions don't have to be negative. You can share fun, happiness and joy in the office through humor. Levity can be a source of positive emotions shared between you and your team, cubicle mates, manager, and customers.

---

1 See *Let the Good Times Roll*.
2 I heard a coworker say this once. She did go to another pre-meeting but luckily she did not die.

Humor and Relationships

Whether it's doing an icebreaker for a new team or sharing a story with just one other person, humor can help foster and strengthen relationships. Humor helps build rapport and trust among individuals and groups and also makes your day a little more fun.

For this book, we're going to think about relationships in the context of how they are created, built, and maintained, as defined below:

- **Icebreakers** – Activities used to help make introductions, to turn strangers into acquaintances.
- **Networking** – Activities used to further introductions beyond a one-time meeting, turning acquaintances into contacts.
- **Community Building** – Activities used to build the overall sense of community within a large group of people or company.
- **Team-Building** – Activities used to build the relationships within a team to improve overall effectiveness through strengthened personal connections.
- **1on1** – Activities used at the most intimate level, helping to build and continue a relationship once it has been established.

With these contexts in mind, here are 100 ways to use humor to build relationships.

ICEBREAKERS

"If you think it's hard to meet new people, try picking up the wrong golf ball."
- Jack Lemmon

People often have a desire to get to know others, especially at events or conferences, but not everyone is naturally extroverted and willing to go and talk to a stranger. Icebreakers remove any social awkwardness from introductions because it "forces" people to meet each other and gives them an excuse to talk.

Humor is a great way to encourage introductions. It creates an initial positive shared experience, laying the foundation for a positive shared relationship.[1]

---

1 And even if people hate the icebreaker, they'll still have developed a relationship... it's virtually fail-proof.

101. Line Up

Hold a team "Line Up" where people line up according to various criteria to facilitate new introductions.

The instructions for the activity follow:

- Participants will form a series of single-file lines, standing in order according to the specified criteria.
- The designated starting and ending points for each line will span the length of the room.
- There may be additional challenges included.

Example line-ups and extra challenges:
- Distance between current location and their birthplace.
- Years of service at organization. Challenge: No talking.
- Height. Challenge: Eyes must be closed.

102. Find Five

Have everyone in the group find either 5 people they have one thing in common with, or one person they have 5 things in common with[1].

103. Hit the Deck

Pass out playing cards. Have all of the cards of the same suit (Hearts, Clubs, etc.) or same rank (King, Queen, blah blah blah) get together and introduce themselves.

104. Assign Seats

At a dinner where people won't know each other, assign seats based on any criteria you know about them. Challenge the people to figure out why they were seated together.

105. Badge Names with Humor

Always create name badges for groups of 20 or more people. Have each person write a fun fact about themselves on the badge.

---

1 For me, I try to find 5 people who love candy as they're likely to have some on them.

106. Say Hello

Try to say hello to every person at an event. No need for a long conversation (but if it happens, great!). Just say, "Hello."

107. Google Someone

Have a computer available for people to Google each other (or themselves)[1].

108. Guess the Person

One person asks a "get to know you" question and everyone writes their answer on a sheet of paper. The asker collects the answers, reads them aloud, and the group guesses who wrote each response.

109. Question Questions

Require people to answer a simple question about themselves whenever asking a question in a group setting.[2]

---

1 If you're going to do this, I recommend letting the people know beforehand. Some people don't like to be surprised when they're going to be Googled all night.
2 "I'll answer your question on the economy in just a second, but first, what's your favorite number?"

110. Question the Kick-off

Start your next meeting with everyone answering the same get-to-know-you question.

Some examples of my favorite questions include[1]:

If you had to change your name, what would you change it to?
What was the first thing you bought with your own money?
What was the last movie/show that made you tear up?
If you could learn any new skill, what would it be?
What is the #1 most played song on your iPod?
What do you want to be when you grow up?
What is one of your favorite quotations?
Who is your celebrity doppelgänger?
What's your favorite time of day?
Where in the heck is Waldo?[2]

---

1 If you want a list of 50 awesome questions, go to htww.co/50q.
2 I have no clue where he is, but did you notice the paragraph shape? See #82.

111. Phone Up Some Pictionary

Play telephone pictionary.

Here's how[1]: First, give everyone in the group a stack of paper with as many sheets as there are people (so if 8 people, everyone gets 8 sheets of paper). Next, tell them:

1. Write your favorite phrase on the top sheet of paper.
2. Pass your entire paper stack to the person on your left.
3. Look at the phrase on the stack handed to you. Move that sheet to the back of the stack and draw a picture representing that phrase on the next sheet of paper.
4. Pass the entire stack to the person on your left.
5. Look at the drawing, move the sheet to the back of the stack and write a sentence describing the picture.
6. Repeat, alternating between writing and drawing until the stacks go all the way around the circle.
7. Spread out the sheets in your stack. Create a story based on the images and phrases (or just see what people did).[2]

---

1 For slides you can use when doing this with a group, go to htww.co/telepict.
2 You can also encourage people to write their names down on the drawings they do. This creates a "business card" the participants can take with them.

112. Improvise

Play improv games with the group[1].

113. Be Diverse

Play *Diversity Bingo* at your next team gathering. Create a Bingo card with various criteria (such as "Owns at least 1 pet" or "Lived outside of this country" and have people mark each box as they meet people who match the criteria.

114. Lie

Play *Two Truths and a Lie* for introductions at your next meeting. Each person says 3 things about themselves, 2 being true, 1 being a lie. Everyone tries to guess which one is the lie.

115. Admit Something You Haven't Done

Play *Never Have I Ever* during the break of a meeting. Everyone takes turns saying something they've never done. Whoever has done it, puts one finger down (or takes a drink[2]). The last person with fingers still up "wins."

1 For a list of improv games, check out: htww.co/improv.
2 Of water or juice of course.

116. Zombify

Warm up your next offsite with *Zombie Tag*[1].

Instructions are simple:

- Everyone in the group mills about the space.
- At some point, you call out someone's name. Anyone with that name instantly becomes a zombie, meaning:
  - Their arms go up in front of them.
  - They walk slower.
  - They say "Braaaaaaiiiiiiiinnnnnnnnssssssss."
- If, while walking, a person gets tagged by a zombie, they also become a zombie.
- The game ends when everyone has become a zombie.
- Note: There is no safety in this world; it's just about seeing how long you'd survive in a zombie apocalypse.

---

1 To see video of this in action, visit htww.co/zombietag.

NETWORKING

"It's not who you know, it's whom."
- Joan Rivers

To some people, networking is a bad word. To others, they see it as how business gets done. While it's true "schmoozers" are a bane to building effective relationships, good networking is about establishing and strengthening individual relationships that are mutually beneficial.

Humor can help facilitate new interactions and set the stage for positive, supportive networking. Plus it reminds both parties that they are talking to a human being, not a robot[1].

---

1 Robots rarely have a sense of humor, unless it's Bender from *Futurama*.

117. Network with Speed

Set up a Speed Networking event. It's the same as speed
dating, but with the intent of networking instead[1].

All you need is 30 minutes, an open space, and people:

1. Ring a bell. Everyone then has 5 minutes to talk to
    someone they've never met, learn about what they do,
    and share a little bit about themselves.
2. After 5 minutes, ring the bell again. People find
    someone else they've never met and start sharing.
3. Lather, rinse, repeat.

*Tip: Encourage people to exchange business cards. Tell them
to write down one thing they learned about the person who
gave it to them. For fun questions to share, see #110.*

---

1 Though you'll generally want to avoid going in for a kiss when networking.

118. Raffle Off Business Cards

Have a bowl to collect business cards. Randomly draw a business card out to decide who you go for a coffee break with[1].

119. Get LinkedIn

Create a LinkedIn group for your company. Encourage people to join, discuss, and give each other recommendations.

120. Get Hip to Facebook

Create a Facebook group for people at your work. Use it to connect socially and share ideas on fun things to do in town[2].

121. Physicalize Facebook

Create a company face book—not the website this time, the original physical copy of pictures, information, and personal details. Make it available for people to skim through (or make it readable on computers and iPads).

---

1 Or who wins a free Chipotle burrito.
2 It also gives you an opportunity to ask people about their experiences. "Hey Jonathan, I saw you went to a Justin Bieber concert. How was that?"

122. Play Halloween

Set out a bowl of candy at your cube; allow people to have a piece only after they tell you a story or make you laugh.[1]

123. Sport Some Friendly Competition

Hold interdepartmental softball, flag football, or soccer (the other kind of football) games. Create teams with people from different work groups or departments to encourage interaction.

124. Be Happy for 60 Minutes

Organize a happy hour with your coworkers[2].

125. Dine Together

Go to lunch with someone new each day for a week. Read *Never Eat Alone* by Keith Ferrazzi if you're curious as to why.

---

1 Are you technically bribing people to come talk to you? Yes, in fact, depending on what kind of candy you have, you could be giving them up to *100 Grand*.
2 Control your drinking, though. You don't want "Happy Hour" to turn into "Got-black-out-drunk-and-said-inappropriate-things-to-my-boss Hour."

126. Greet, Meet, Eat

Start a lunch bunch.

I first started this at *P&G* and it was a great success[1]. It didn't cost the company any money and employees were already going to lunch—it just added some networking.

Setting it up is easy—just collect a list of people who are interested in participating and, once a month, send out new groupings of who goes to lunch together. The group decides when and where (with packing lunch an option).[2]

Though it's simple to do, the results are far from trivial. Here's what some people said about the bunch I led:

- *"I've made some great connections with people and received some priceless advice."*
- *"[It's] an opportunity to get to know the people I work with."*
- *"[I] feel more like a neighbor."*

---

1 Though I started it in New York, by the time I left, I knew of at least 4 other "lunch bunch" groups from around the world.
2 Mary Kay Morrison, Director at *Humor Quest*, recommends something similar, except instead of getting together for lunch, her bunches get together for a fun activity. Find out more about Mary Kay at www.humorquest.com.

77

127. Read and Discuss

Start a business (or fiction) book club at work.

Some of my favorite business books include[1]:

- *Getting Things Done* by David Allen
- *How to Win Friends and Influence People* by Dale Carnegie
- *Seven Habits of Highly Effective People* by Stephen Covey
- *The Effective Executive* by Peter Drucker
- *The Levity Effect* by Adrian Gostick and Scott Christopher
- *The Personal MBA* by Josh Kaufman
- *The 80/20 Principle* by Richard Koch
- *Brain Rules* by John Medina
- *22 Immutable Laws of Marketing* by Al Reis & Jack Trout
- *On Writing Well* by William Zinsser

---

1 I learned many of these from PersonalMBA.com. The site, run by Josh Kaufman (a former *P&G* colleague), is dedicated to helping readers educate themselves on advanced business concepts without spending gobs of money on an MBA. His book, *The Personal MBA,* is an international bestseller.

128. Exchange

Organize a book or DVD exchange between coworkers. Have people share reviews of the products they are exchanging.

129. Piece It Together

Put out a jigsaw puzzle in the breakroom for people to work on together during a break[1].

130. Play Your Heart Out

Set up the video game *Rock Band* (or a similar game). Allow people to create "Bands" that play during lunch.

131. Cook Up Some Connections

Organize trips to a local college or school (or bring teachers into the office) for employees to attend classes on personal life skills, such as a cooking or beer brewing class[2].

---

1 If you want to evil about it, get a puzzle that's all sky or has no edge pieces.
2 Brewing beer probably isn't a necessary personal life skill, but people tell me it's fun. I personally like to "brew" my own chocolate milk flavors. Extra chocolate is the best.

132. Give Back

Encourage employees to volunteer at local charities, either as individuals or as a group, by awarding time off for giving back. Not only will they meet new people, they'll also be happier (which is a plus for the company).

Who says they'll be happier? Psychologists and researchers[1]:

- People who committed random acts of kindness felt happier for weeks after the act.[2]
- Neurologically, giving money to charity activates the same reward centers of the brain as doing cocaine.[3]
- Giving = Happiness is universal. Data from 136 countries showed that spending money on others and happiness is correlated.[4]

---

1 For even more on this, see *Optimal Philanthropy for Human Beings.*
2 See *Pursuing sustained happiness.*
3 See *Neural responses to giving.*
4 See *Prosocial spending and well-being.*

COMMUNITY BUILDING

Jeff: "Helping only ourselves is bad and helping each other is good."
- Community, Season 3

If you want your organization to have a strong sense of loyalty, you have to provide opportunities for everyone in the organization to feel like they are part of something bigger than just their job or team. Strong communities lead to happier and healthier lives and they create a more stable and supportive environment.[1]

Humor can help you build your corporate community and create a culture of creativity, spontaneity, support, and fun.

---

1 See *The Importance of Community.*

133. Hire Paparazzi

Hire a photographer to take pictures of an event (or just show up on a normal day in the office). Hold a meeting to share a slideshow of the pictures.

134. Scavenge for Fun

Have employees participate in an *Amazing Race*-like scavenger hunt. Include challenges that involve taking pictures or video of them doing fun activities[1]. Share the media after the hunt is over.

135. Party without a Plan

Hold an "impromptu" office party. Have people bring cheap office supplies from their desk as gifts.

136. Unleash Your Inner Village Person

Perform the YMCA at your next community meeting.[2]

---

1 One of my favorite activities I've done on such a hunt was make a quick commercial for a local business. Not only did we have fun, we also got a free sandwich out of it.
2 Or create a parody of it. I've sung versions titled: PSAT, OGSM and DREW.

137. Tape Up Some Fashion

Have a Duct Tape Fashion Show.[1]

Assemble everyone into teams. Supply each team with rolls of duct tape of various colors. Have each team create an outfit from their tape. After construction is over, host a fashion show where each team wears their creation and walks down a runway in front of their peers.

I did this once with a community of engineers and project managers—stereotypically not your biggest group of fashion–focused individuals. But as soon as the contest started, it was like *America's Next Top Model*.

They drew up fashion designs, created elaborate costumes complete with accessories and logos, and strutted their stuff down the runway. The event was a huge success.

---

1 For pictures of incredible costumes made of duct tape, see htww.co/duct.

138. Tailgate with Coworkers

Have a tailgate party in your work parking lot. Use it to celebrate a big event or to offset the inconvenience of people having to come into the office over the weekend.

139. Get Lucky

Organize a potluck lunch with people in your office.

140. Cook for Success

Have upper management (or project leaders) cook a meal for everyone when big goals are achieved[1].

141. Prove You've Got Talent

Hold a talent show. Ask employees to share their unique talents in front of their peers. Solicit talents like singing, dancing, stand-up comedy, spinning plates, or really really really fast typing.[2]

---

1 The meal doesn't have to be elaborate, people just enjoy seeing their managers in a servant role / wearing a sweet chef's hat.
2 According to the *Guinness Book of World Records*, the fastest recorded typing speed is 212 wpm, held by Barbara Blackburn on a Dvorak keyboard.

142. Make Up Talent

If you don't think you have talent (trust me you do), or you want to get people out of their heads, hold an improvised talent show.

Here's how:

- Organize people into teams.
- Give a set amount of time (30 to 45 minutes) for each team to come up with a skit, song, or other type of performance that they will present to the group.
- After the planning time is over, host a talent show as normal, with each group performing.
- At the end, decide a winner.[1]

A few helpful tips:
- Require everyone in the group to be involved in the performance in some way.
- Set minimum/maximum time limits for each performance.
- For additional challenge, you can require each team to include a particular phrase or word in the show.

---

1 Hint: The winner is usually everyone because they all tend to be hilarious.

143. Attract Poetry

Buy refrigerator poetry magnets for the lunchroom.

144. Get Cartoony

Start a "Humor Me" board where people can post funny cartoons, quotations, or short stories they find in the newspaper or online.[1]

145. Post a Bulletin

Put a bulletin board in a common area like the lunchroom; take turns with your coworkers posting different topics on the board. Encourage them to post semi-work-related topics, like tips for work/life balance or something awesome like how to use humor in the workplace.[2]

146. Paint Together

Have a "mural" wall or canvas where people can come together to paint a mural (or just random images) together.

1 Hat tip to Tony Q, an office manager at a science and technology company, for the suggestion. As Tony said, "Some folks are not good at telling jokes, but they are more than willing to share something humorous if they saw it someplace."
2 I had to do these as a RA. They can be great way to educate AND generate discussion.

147. Showcase Your Kids

Create a "look at what my kid made" exhibit for employees to share their kids' creations[1].

148. Capture Cute Babies

Have an "I Was a Cute Baby Contest" where everyone brings in pictures of themselves as kids. Post them on a board along with pictures of what the people look like now.

149. Bring Your X to Work

Encourage people to participate in Bring Your Kid (or Spouse (or Pet)) to Work Day.[2]

150. Host Family Holidays

Allow family members to come in on holidays like Halloween. Pass out candy to the kids (and adults).

---

1 My mom still has the ceramic swan I made her 15+ years ago. Awwww.
2 For a list of dates, go to htww.co/xtowork. FYI: Bring your Teddy Bear to Work is on the Second Wednesday in October.

151. Celebrate Half–Holidays

Have "Holiday" parties six months from their actual date: Halloween in April, an indoor luau in December.

Alternatively, you can also celebrate half–birthdays (the date six months before/after someone's actual birthday).

Here are the dates for some good Half–Holidays:

Half 4th of July – January 4th
Half Halloween – April 30th
Half Thanksgiving – 4th Thursday of May
Half St. Patrick's Day – September 17th
Half Start of Summer – December 22nd

152. Recognize

Send out a quarterly recognition email recognizing the accomplishments of fellow employees and sharing some humor.

153. Give Kudos

Have a "Kudos" board at your next offsite. Get an envelope for every attendee, lots of blank postcards, and pens. Encourage people to write quick handwritten "thank yous" to their coworkers and place them in their envelope.[1]

154. Celebrate Coworker's Day

Host an employee appreciation day in the vein of Mother's Day or Father's Day where anyone can celebrate anyone else.

155. Award Humor

Include "Humor Awards" at your next offsite. Solicit nominations for awards in categories like best email, best meeting, best video, and best offsite.

---

1 It was through one of these boards that I learned people really like my hair.

156. Customize Humor Awards

Allow people to create "Custom Humor Awards" for your next award ceremony. They come up with the name of the award, the "criteria," and the winner.

Here are some example awards that have been "won":

- The *Not in My House* Award.
  For: Someone not afraid of saying no to scope creep.
- The *Most Likely to Answer a Question with a Story* Award.
  For: Someone who always uses stories to answer questions.
- The *Can't Turn Off Work* Award.
  For: Someone who leverages corporate buzzwords when dialoguing with friends and family.
- The *Booty Call* Award.
  For: Someone who has, on more than one occasion, accidentally butt–dialed a coworker.
- The *He Thinks He's Punny* Award.
  For: Someone who uses puns in their emails.[1]

---

1 I may have been the recipient of this award...

TEAM BUILDING

"A group is a bunch of people in an elevator. A team is also a bunch of people in an elevator, but the elevator is broken."
- Bonnie Edelstein

The most productive teams are those who know each other. Team members who know each other's strengths, weaknesses, and preferred working style are more productive and have higher job satisfaction[1].

Humor can help create strong teams with members who leverage each other's strengths, account for each other's weaknesses, and actually enjoy working together.

---

1 See *Teamwork and Job Satisfaction.*

157. Gift Gifted Gift-Certificates

Hand out gift certificates for a job well done... with the caveat that the gift certificate can't be used for themselves but for a coworker they think was instrumental in helping them.

Why does this work?[1]

1. Organizations that give regular thanks for their employees outperform those that don't.
2. Companies with a "recognition–rich–culture" have a 31% lower voluntary turnover rate.
3. Top–down recognition is seen as political; peer-to-peer recognition feels more meaningful.

---

1 See *Secret of Employee Recognition.*

158. End with Cheer

End every status meeting with someone giving a "shout-out" to a team-member for something they did.

159. Get Animated

Create Simpson's avatars for all of your team members[1].

160. Become Royalty

Find out which Disney Princess you are[2]; watch the movie starring whichever princess is most prevalent in your team.

161. Create Project Codenames

Create project-specific nicknames or call signs for members of your team. If you can't think of any good nicknames, find out their Pirate name or create an anagram out of their full name.[3]

---

1 Go to htww.co/simpsons to access the avatar generator.
2 Take the quiz at htww.co/princess.
3 Anagrams of Andrew Tarvin: Drawn Air Vent, Rad Raven Twin, Vain Wart Nerd.

162. Shake Hands Secretly

Create a secret handshake for members of your team. It can be simple as "hitting the rock" or as complex as "rocking the baby."[1]

163. ID Your Team

For teams that last longer than 6 months, create Membership Cards for each member. Require them for entry into meetings.

164. Have a Team Name

Name your row of cubicles something indicative of the people or work done there; encourage others to do the same[2].

165. Add a Button

Order buttons with your project team name or logo and give them out to resources who help you.

---

1 For inspiration, check out this list of great handshakes: htww.co/handshakes.
2 My first role at *P&G* was in Modeling & Simulation. Each of our cubicles was named after a different type of model: hand, hair, hip, etc.

166. Make Your Team Super

Photoshop pictures of your team onto pictures of super heroes, celebrities or historical figures.

Isaac Drewton

167. Find a Pin-Up

Make a calendar full of pictures of people from your department. Pick a theme (like Firefighter Calendar) for the pin-up.

168. Bobble Your Heads

Get bobbleheads made of your team members.

169. Assign Coworker Superlatives

Include "senior superlatives" as part of your project closure celebration. Some example superlatives: Best Hair, Best Dressed, Most Likely to Use Punctuation, Corporate Joker[1].

170. Decorate

Make thematic "door decs" (craft-like signs you can hang on the office door or cubicle wall) for the people on your team.[2]

---

1 I was once the winner of "Most Likely to Eat Pop Tarts for Breakfast." I was proud.
2 This also comes from my time as an RA. If you lack the necessary craft skills, like I did, find someone who knows what they're doing and barter for their services.

171. Author-ize

Work with coworkers to write a book about your workplace. Use a service like WeBook to create it[1].

172. Hit the Bar

Hold a Friday afternoon meeting at a bar. It can encourage new ways of thinking, loosen people up, and build relationships.[2]

173. Rotate Facilitators

For regularly scheduled meetings, rotate who the facilitator is and encourage everyone to add their own style when it's their turn.

174. Huddle Up

Huddle up with your team at the beginning or end of meetings. Actually get in a football-like huddle and give a quick "pep" talk[3].

---

1 Find more info at www.webook.com.
2 Jamie Rollins, an office administrator working in mobile advertising, says her company brings the bar to the employees: "Friday at 4:30pm is considered Beer:Thirty."
3 "OK, Steve, you run a hook pattern to the copy machine to pick up the print-outs. Sarah, you run a slant to book the boardroom. Tim, you do the blocking in case the project board calls a blitz of scope creep. Alright, break!"

175. Map and Match

Gather trivia about the people on your team—send out a mapping and matching quiz and see who can correctly guess all of the matches.

From doing this, I learned that I worked with someone who[1]:

- Is an identical quintuplet.
- Was in an MTV Music Video.
- Has appeared on the show Magnum PI.
- Has rappelled off of the Great Wall of China.
- Once had to take a call from Colombian kidnappers (everything turned out OK).

---

1 Note: These are not all the same person, they are separate facts for separate people. Although it's possible that 1 single person has experienced all of these things, I have not met them.

176. Hold a Photo Shoot

Have a fancy photo shoot (or go to Glamour Shots) with your team. Encourage them to dress as fancy as possible.

177. Pool Your Bets

Have office pools for sporting events, but instead of betting money have an inexpensive award that the winner receives[1].

178. Investigate Better Relationships

Play a game like Murder or Mafia[2].

179. Get on the High Ropes

Go to a high ropes course with your team. Encourage everyone to participate, even (especially?) if they are afraid of heights.

---

1 Check your HR policy on this one. I'd hate for you to get in trouble because you bet your boss that if the *Reds* win, you get his parking spot for a month.
2 These are names of games, not things to do or join. Get info at htww.co/mobgames.

180. Be Gross

Hold a "grossest foods" dessert party.

I first learned this way back in the 5th Grade from my math teacher. Once a semester, all of the kids brought in any snack–like food they wanted. Items included:

Oreos, Pop Tarts, Gummy Worms, Fruit by the Foot, Nerds, Marshmallows, Peanuts, Doritos, Crackers, Salsa, Ketchup, Mayonnaise, and Sardines[1].

The contest was simple. Try to create the "grossest" combination of the above foods. After the masterpieces were assembled, the class voted on the grossest "recipe" and, if you ate it AND kept the food down, you won.[2]

Every time we did it, the teacher was the winner. He would just take a little bit of everything and gulp it down. I don't know how he did it.

---

1 I don't know what kid snacks on sardines, but I guess it happens.
2 I don't remember now what you actually won. Pride, maybe?

1-ON-1

"Just the two of us."
- *Grover Washington Jr.*
- *Bill Withers*
- *Will Smith*

Relationships ultimately come down to the one-on-one interactions between two people. The conversations, activities, and discussions two individuals have together help to sustain and continue the relationship. When all of that goes away, the relationship starts to deteriorate.

Using humor can be a great way to connect on a human-to-human level that builds and maintains important relationships.

181. Remember Names

Do whatever is necessary to remember people's names[1].

As Dale Carnegie notes: "A person's name is, to that person, the sweetest and most important sound in any language."

How do you do it? Here are a few tips:

- When you first meet someone, try to use their name at least three times while talking with them.
- Use a mnemomic device of alliteration or rhyme.
- Create a mental image of their name attached to a detail about them.
- Write it down (on paper, in your phone, on your hand...)
- Ask if you've forgotten.[2]

---

1 Saying you're "bad with names" isn't a good excuse. Practice.
2 It's much better to ask someone their name instead of just referring to them as "Hey You," or avoiding them altogether because you're embarrassed.

182. Distribute Headshots

Print out headshots of yourself (or famous people) and autograph them with personal messages for your coworkers.

183. Track Your Contacts

Create a "Contacts" folder in your email. Whenever news of promotions or personal successes about your contacts come via email, put it in that folder.

184. Add Context to Contacts

Remember details about people you want a close relationship with, even if "remembering" means writing things down[1].

185. Say Happy Birthday

Acknowledge people's birthdays, either by having cake, or just saying it to them. Use Facebook as a last resort.[2]

---

1 Some people are great at remembering details about their contacts. Some are not. Just because you don't have a good memory doesn't mean it's not important.
2 Just be careful of singing them the Birthday Song in public. Technically it's copyrighted until at least the year 2030.

186. Game Online

Play *Words with Friends* or *Scramble* with coworkers.[1]

187. Have Tea Time

Spice up your normal coffee break by going out for "tea time" instead. Drink out of fancy tea cups.[2]

188. Fool in April

Pull a harmless (keyword: harmless) April Fool's Joke on a good coworker. Make sure it's not anything that causes permanent damage (physical or mental).[3]

189. Be a Secret Interior Decorator

Modify something at a coworkers desk (such as rearranging items on their desk or turning their photos upside down). See how long it takes them to notice.

---

1 These games and more are available on both iOS and Android platforms.
2 Also, I believe, pinkies should be up.
3 Hat tip to Bradley Zangel for the following suggestion: get some party poppers and attach them to a coworker's cupboard or drawer so that it POPS when they open it.

190. Unlock Desktop Fun

If a coworker leaves their computer unlocked while they are away, make a quick change to their computer as "punishment" for leaving the company "at risk".

Some good quick changes[1]:

- Change their desktop background to an image from a kid's TV show such as *My Little Ponies*.
- Switch to "High Contrast Mode" on the computer to invert the color-scheme of the monitor.
- Change the orientation of the screen so that it displays the desktop upside down.
- Turn on "Toggle Keys" which makes the computer beep every time you press a lock key.

---

1 The computer shortcuts for these can be found at htww.co/prankkeys. Use them at your own risk.

191. Be Ambient Aware

Befriend a good coworker on Facebook and/or follow them on Twitter.

This type of social networking allows for ambient awareness, or "awareness created through regular and constant reception, and/or exchange of information fragments through social media."[1] The NY Times likens it to "being physically near someone and picking up on mood through little things; body language, sights, stray comments..."[2]

Why would you want that? Users of social media suggest that this ambient awareness brings them closer together with more people and limited extra work.

---

1 See *Ambient awareness.*
2 See *Brave New World of Digital Intimacy.*

192. Re-connect

Call an old colleague or manager just to reconnect. Ask how they are doing and give them an update on you.

193. Question the Cubicle

Ask a coworker about the things in their cubicle or office, such as the pictures they put up, awards they display, or desktop background they have on their computer[1].

194. Share Personal Achievements

Make sure part of your 1-on-1 is devoted to both people sharing a recent personal achievement or event. It could be about anything, so long as it's not about work.

195. Be a Freshmaker

Find a mentor; give them *Mentos* for mentoring.[2]

---

1 It's also good to personalize your own cubicle so people can learn more about you.
2 Check out htww.co/mentos for a good frame of reference.

196. High Five

Give people high fives when you pass them in the hallway.

197. Say Thank You

Send a thank you note at least once a week. It could be for something big (like giving you guidance on a career decision) or small (like helping you book a conference room).[1]

198. Start a Slow Clap

Be the person that starts an applause for someone.[2] Alternatively, give someone a standing ovation for something. Anything (at the end of a presentation, closing a deal, for just being them).

199. Praise Others

Send a coworker anonymous praise.

---

1 You should do this because it lets the other person know they are valued, but it also helps you out. It often makes you feel good and that person will remember your gratitude and is likely to be willing to help you out again in the future.
2 If all works out well, it'll be like the "slow clap" in the movies.

200. Learn the Language

If you work internationally, learn a few words and phrases from the primary language of one of your coworkers. Surprise them with your new vocabulary in your next meeting.

Some key phrases to learn (plus how to say them in another language):

Hello.[1]	*Privet.* (Russian)
Goodbye.	*Elveda.* (Turkish)
Thank you.	*Grazzi.* (Maltese)
Please.	*Baal ma.* (Wolof)
I'm sorry.	*Choe-song-ham-ni-da.* (Korean)
Where is the bathroom?	*¿Dónde está el baño?* (Spanish)
Happy Birthday.	*qoSlIj DatIvjaj* (Klingon)

---

1 For even more ways to say hello, check out #13.

SKILL #3:
PROBLEM SOLVING

Problem Solving is a critical skill for success in business—in fact it's often what you're hired and paid to do. Humor can help in each of the steps, not only by boosting creativity but also increasing the enjoyment of work.

If a problem is "a state of desire for reaching a definite goal from a present condition,"[1] problem solving is "the management of a problem in a way that successfully meets the goals established for treating it."[2] Successfully solving a problem doesn't necessarily mean it has completely gone away, it just means you've achieved your goal with regard to the issue.

Said differently, solving a problem is an opportunity to move from your current state to a more ideal state. As Henry J. Kaiser said, "Problems are only opportunities in work clothes."

---

1 See *Problem solving.*
2 See *Introduction to Problem Solving.*

Problem Solving and Doors

Sometimes problems are huge undertakings requiring lots of time, planning, and resources. Other times, they are as simple as a locked door. Such was the case when I was presenting on problem solving for the first time. It was at a conference with various break–outs, including my own on *The 5 Steps to Improvised Problem Solving.*

I was all set to give my presentation, but as I arrived a few minutes early to set up the room, I found the door was locked. Then people started showing up, accumulating in the hallway, waiting to learn about problem solving.

A quick pass through the first four steps of problem solving had me running to a moderator in another break–out, informing them of the situation. They called the custodial staff to unlock the door and I went back to the hallway, now filled with attendees, and started my introduction (why waste time?). By the time I got through the equivalent of the first slide of my presentation, a custodian came and unlocked the door.

We filed into the room and I resumed my presentation, joking that "I staged the whole thing to demonstrate problem solving in action."

Evaluating things later, going through the steps and maintaining a sense of humor about the whole situation led to a better real–life example than I ever could have imagined.

Humor and Problem Solving

Humor and creativity go together like two "p's" in a "ppod"[1]. Both involve looking at two things and seeing how they can come together in a new way[2]. That creativity helps solve problems.

For the purposes of this book, we're going to think about how humor applies to the five steps of problem solving, as defined below:

- **Problem Definition** – Defining the problem you are attempting to solve in such a way that you can take action on finding a solution.
- **Brainstorming** – Generating a large list of ideas from which the solution will be selected.
- **Decision Making** – Analyzing the list of ideas and identifying the best solution.
- **Implementation** – Putting the solution into place.
- **Evaluation** – Evaluating the solution and determining any additional steps needed.

With these contexts in mind, here are 100 ways to use humor to enhance problem solving.

---

1 I've never understand that expression. What's a ppod?
2 See *Laughing All the Way to the Bank.*

PROBLEM DEFINITION

"Everything should be as simple as it can be, but not simpler."
- *Albert Einstein*

How you define a problem can go a long way in determining how you *solve* the problem. Establishing a goal—and not just stating what's wrong—better defines what you're attempting to achieve and helps you know whether or not you've been successful in your pursuit.

Humor can help you come up with a problem definition that not only helps you solve the right problem, but one that is exciting to work on.

201. Want It

Create a "Wanted" poster for a problem to be resolved. Describe the attributes of the problem and list what the reward is for catching the "scoundrel."

202. Make a Supervillain

Imagine the problem is a supervillain in a comic book.[1] What is its superpower? What does it wear? Who is the hero?

203. Go Hollywood

Pretend your problem is the plot of a movie. What's the title? Who are the lead actors (hero and villain)? Who's the director?

204. Sing the Problem

Write the lyrics of a rap or country song where your problem is the subject of the song[2]. Bonus points if you perform the song.

205. Anthropomorphize the Problem

Think about your problem as if it were a creature of some sort. Draw an anatomy diagram that represents the legs, arms, heart, and brain of the problem.

---

1 "Oh no, it's Shrinking Budget Man. Ahhhhhhh!"
2 Our software is buggy, making it slow. / The customers are jailed, they cannot pass go.

206. Picture the Problem

Find an image that seems to represent the problem. Try to find an image that could represent the solution.

207. Storm the Words

Use a "wordstorm" to see how the problem links to other ideas[1].

208. Celebrate in the Future

Imagine it's 1 year in the future, write down what you'd like to be celebrating. What looks like success a year from now?[2]

209. Yell Your Problem

Take turns saying (in a louder than normal voice) "You know what your problem is..." and then defining the problem you are trying to solve.

---

1 Go to htww.co/wordstorm to find out more.
2 For example, a year from now, I'd like to be a year older. Fingers crossed.

210. Decide What Else is True

Apply the improv principle "If this is true, what else is true" to your problem. Use it to generate thoughts on all aspects of the problem, not just the immediately obvious.

If this is true, what else is true comes from the *Upright Citizen's Brigade*, an improv theater and training center with locations in New York and Los Angeles.

In improv, the idea is that if you've established something is true in a scene (e.g., there's been a zombie apocalypse), you can generate comedy by thinking about what else would be true (e.g., the zombies would have to get jobs).

In problem solving, this concept can help you better define your goal. If I'm a zombie and need a job, what else is true? Well I am a zombie, so my reaction time is slower and I have bad motor skills. Also I need money, so I probably have a certain kind of lifestyle I need to support. So I don't just need a job. I need a job that covers my expenses, is OK if I move slowly, and doesn't require much brainpower. I need to be a congressman.[1]

1 Oh, buurrrnnn. I'm kidding, I appreciate the hard work some of them do.

211. Put on a Hat

Think about a problem while wearing different hats (figuratively, or literally if you'd like); have each hat represent a different mindset, such as de Bono's six thinking hats[1].

212. Talk to Strangers

Talk to a complete stranger about the problem (in general terms). Try Chat Roulette[2] or a forum to find the stranger.

213. Solve Like I'm Five

Explain the problem like you were talking to a 5 year old. Think about how a 5 year old would solve it[3].

214. Acronym One Word

Decide on one word to represent your problem. Make an acronym out of that word further defining it. For example, TIRED = Time Indicating Rest is an Encroaching Desire.

---

1 Not to be confused with the lead singer of *U2*, Edward de Bono defined six distinct directions in which the brain can be challenged. Check out htww.co/debono for more.
2 Be very careful as Chat Roulette is not always Safe-For-Work.
3 See #51 for more information.

215. Cut in Half

Write the problem down in 40 words or less. Now 20 words or less. Now 10 words. Now 5.

216. Headline the Problem

Write the problem statement as if it were a headline in *The New York Times* or *The Onion*[1].

217. Define with Mad Libs

Turn your problem statement into a Mad Lib (also known as a "phrasal template"). Get different people to fill it out and find the best description.

218. Get Attracted to Poetry

Go the breakroom and use poetry magnets to artfully define your problem.[2]

---

1 *The Onion* is a satirical website that creates fake news, with stories like: *Archaeological Dig Uncovers Ancient Race of Skeleton People*. Find more at htww.co/onion.
2 See #143

219. Redefine Your Language

Use an automated translator to translate your problem statement into another language. And then back to the original language[1].

Original: A train leaves Chicago for Detroit going 60 mph. At the same time, on an adjacent track, a train leaves Detroit heading for Chicago going 45 mph. Detroit is 280 miles from Chicago. How far are the trains from Chicago when they pass?

Bulgarian: Влакът напуска Чикаго за Детройт ще 60 mph. В същото време, на съседен път, влакът напуска Детройт позиция за Чикаго става 45 mph. Детройт е на 280 мили от Чикаго. Колко далеч са влаковете от Чикаго, когато те минават?

English Again: The train left Chicago to Detroit to 60 mph. Meanwhile, on a nearby road, train leaves Chicago Detroit position to 45 mph. Detroit is 280 miles from Chicago. How far are the trains from Chicago when they pass?

---

1 You can do this translation back and forth as many times as you want.

BRAINSTORMING

---

*"Think left and think right
and think low and think high.
Oh, the thinks you can think up
if only you try!"*
                    - Dr. Seuss

The process of generating ideas and solutions comes naturally to some and seemingly not at all to others. Brainstorming is a way to generate a number of ideas, with the hope that the solution lies within. However, not all brainstorming is created equal, sometimes bearing no fruitful possibilities.

Humor can help improve the range of ideas included in brainstorming sessions and get participants to think outside the proverbial box.

220. Yes And

Before focusing on what's wrong with an idea, practice "Yes And" and focus on what's right with an idea.

Yes And comes from improvisation, and, at its core, is about accepting an idea (*yes*) and building on it (*and*).

Both elements are equally important. The *yes* doesn't mean you agree with an idea, merely that you accept it as being offered. The *and* takes what you like about the offer and adds something else, continuing to progress the idea.

Notice how different this is from the traditional work phrases of *No Because,* where you say no and explain what's wrong, or *Yes But*, where technically you say yes but then still explain what's wrong. This type of mindset is too obsessed with what *is* instead of what *could be*.

Instead, focus on opportunities and think *Yes And*[1].

---

1 In fact there's an exercise called *Yes And* you can specifically use. Start brainstorming out loud. After each idea, the next person who speaks says "Yes, and..." then adds something to the idea.

221. Look for the Dumb

Start a brainstorming session by trying to get the "dumbest" ideas out first. Keep a list of the really bad (and really good) ones.

222. Post–It Note–It

Have people write ideas down on post–it notes at the start to eliminate the fear of being connected to a "stupid" idea.

223. Humor the Brain

Enhance creativity by watching 20 minutes of comedy before starting a brainstorming or critical thinking session[1].

224. Riddle the Brain

Get the brain thinking in different mindsets by answering or reviewing riddles prior to brainstorming.

---

1 In one study, students were split into groups. One group watched a comedy film and one watched a neutral film. They then had to solve a problem. The number of students who successfully solved the problem was 55% higher in the group that watched the comedy film than the neutral one. See *Humor Benefits: Increases Creativity*.

225. Just Think

Block off at least 60 minutes to sit in a room with a pen and some paper and just think.

226. Generate to Music

Listen to music while brainstorming ideas. Let different tracks influence your thinking style[1].

227. Diversify the Thinking

Create a team of diverse people to brainstorm[2]. Look for diversity across age, race, gender, function, experience, and sense of humor.

228. Answer the Woulds

Answer the following: "What would you do if time & money were no object?" "What would you do if you had to solve this in 5 minutes with only $5?" Compare the answers.

---

1 Use Heavy Metal for aggressive ideas, Classical for highbrow, Soundtracks for epic.
2 Studies have shown diverse teams are able to come up with more effective and feasible solutions than a homogeneous team. See *Diversity and Creativity*.

229. Connect Analogies

Try to find a similar problem that's already been solved and reapply the solution to your situation[1].

James Dyson, inventor of the *Dyson Vacuum Cleaner*, developed over 5,100 patents before arriving at the "Root Cyclone" technology used in his products.

Where did the inspiration for Root Cyclone technology come from? A visit to a saw mill, where Dyson noticed that saw dust was being pulled out of the air and collected in a chamber via a large cyclone atop the roof of the mill.

He took this concept of centrifugal force and put it into his vacuum, building a company with over $1 billion in annual sales as a result.[2]

---

1 One specialized field of this is called biomimicry—finding a similar issue in nature and seeing how nature resolved it. Check out htww.co/biomimicry.
2 See *The Man Behind the Vacuum Cleaner*.

230. Ponder WWXD?

Think of great thought leaders, successful entrepreneurs, or even cartoon characters and image what they would do about the problem.

Here's a list of people I've tried to think like[1]:

Socrates	Steve Jobs
Sun Tzu	William Buffet
Benjamin Franklin	Mark Zuckerberg
Abraham Lincoln	Tony Stark
Nikola Tesla	Han Solo
Gandhi	Garfield
Albert Einstein	Bugs Bunny

---

1 Note: You don't have to like or agree with the real-life version of this person, just think about how they might go about solving your problem.

231. Script the Specs

Imagine the problem was the plot of your favorite TV show. What would the episode be like and how would the characters solve the problem?[1]

232. Multiply by 1,000

Imagine your problem is 1,000 times harder, what would you do? And if it were 1,000 times easier?

233. Fill the Gap

Draw a picture of two cliff edges creating a gap. Write down your current state on the left and ideal state on the right. Fill in the gap with words describing what you can do to get there.

234. Autocorrect

Type various ideas into an iPhone or Android phone quickly. Leave any autocorrections in there.

---

1 Bonus points if you submit a "spec script" and end up a full-time writer on the show.

235. Get Definition

Turn to a random page in the dictionary and generate ideas from at least 3 of the words on that page.

236. Alphabetize

Generate an idea that starts with each letter of the alphabet.

237. Rule with 9

Follow the comedy Rule of 9[1] and do a 10x10x10 Matrix. Write a list of 10 ideas. Pick the best idea and write 10 extensions of that one idea. Take one idea from that list and write 10 more extentions of that idea.

238. Pass the Solution

Have everyone write down the first sentence of a possible solution on their own sheet of paper. Have everyone pass their paper to the person sitting next to them, who then writes the next sentence of the solution (and so on and so on)[2].

1 The Rule of 9 in comedy states that 90% of what you write will be crap. This holds true regardless of what level of comedy you are at.
2 Similar to the Telephone Pictionary game described in #111.

239. Get Random Ideas

Hold a virtual brainstorming session. Challenge people to call–in from the most random place they can think of (coffee shop, park, baseball game, etc).

Why? Studies suggest that getting away from the office can spur creativity. One study found that participants were more creative in a bustling coffee shop than in a quiet office, attributing it to distraction. "A moderate distraction, which induces processing difficulty, enhances creativity by prompting abstract thinking."[1]

In his book *Iconoclast*, author Gregory Burns explains, "Sometimes a simple change of environment is enough to jog the perceptual system out of familiar categories... when confronted with places never seen before...the brain jumbles around old ideas with new images to create new syntheses."[2]

---

1 See *Ambient Noise and Creative Cognition*.
2 See *Iconoclast*.

240. Travel to Think

Travel somewhere. Use the time sitting in the car or on the plane to "mull over" the problem.

241. Think on the Go

When thinking through a problem, do a physical activity like walking up stairs or around the office.

242. Sleep On It

Think about the problem before going to bed. Brainstorm ideas the moment you wake up. Incorporate ideas from any dreams you remember.

243. Shower

Shower[1] and see where your mind goes[2].

---

1 Some people say "take a shower," others say "get a shower." I say you can't physically take or get a shower, so why not just "shower?"
2 Showering forces a "creative pause" which, combined with the white noise generated from the water and the distraction of cleaning yourself, can prove a very fertile ground for new ideas. See *Creative pause.*

DECISION MAKING

"Cake or death?"
"Uh, cake please."
"Well, we're out of cake! ..."
"So my choice is 'or death?'"
- Eddie Izzard

The ability to make decisions is critical in the business world. Not only is it the pre–cursor to work actually getting completed, it's also what allows us to go to lunch[1]. When solving problems, making a decision requires analyzing the possible solutions and identifying the best one.

Humor can provide a unique way of looking at what's possible and finding the right solution. Who knew decision making could be so fun?

---

1 Does this sound familiar: "Let's go to lunch." "Sure." "Where do you want to go?" "I don't care." "I don't either." "So where should we go?" "I don't know." SOMEONE JUST MAKE A DECISION (sorry for yelling).

244. Throw Darts

Put a list of ideas on a dart board. Throw a dart to see which of the ideas to explore first.[1]

245. Draw from a Hat

Write down your top ideas on separate pieces of paper, put them in a hat, and pick one out. Discuss why that would or wouldn't be the right solution.

246. Flip a Coin

When deciding between two ideas, flip a coin. The solution isn't what the coin tells you to do, it's what you secretly hope is the result when the coin is in the air.

247. Race the Possibilities

Go to a horse race (or any kind of competition). Assign an idea to each contestant and see which one wins[2].

---

1 You can also reuse the dartboard for #483.

2 Your possible solutions also make for good horse names: "*Increase the Budget* pulls into the lead; he's followed closely by *Cut Scope*. *Do Nothing* is bringing up the rear."

248. Scale the Solution

Draw a scale with each side representing a different idea.
Put the pros on each side and see which idea has more
weight.

Don't Get a Snack

Get a Snack

Sugars
Have to Move

Delicious
Be Happier
Satiates Hunger

249. Battle to the Death

Compare two ideas at random in an "Idea Battle to the Death." Winner takes on the next idea in the next round. The last idea standing, wins.

Deciding Where to Eat:[1]

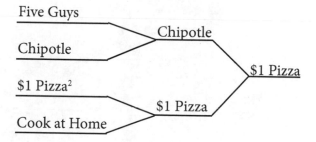

---

1 This is a typical decision I make based on the food options near me.
2 $1 Pizza is a place that sells a NY style slice of pizza for only $1. It's delicious and inexpensive, meaning it's often the winner.

250. Hold a Tournament

Assign each possible solution to a person. Do a *Rock-Paper-Scissors* or *Odds & Evens* tournament to decide the winner.[1]

251. Put on a Trial

Have each idea "stand trial." Select people to be the prosecutor, defense attorney, and judge. Hold 5-minute cases for each idea.

252. Take the Top

Have people anonymously rank their top three ideas. Repeat the process a day or two later and take the highest ranked ideas.

253. Survey Solutions

Create a survey listing possible solutions and have people (coworkers, friends, strangers) rate them. Include an open text box for people to give feedback or submit their own ideas.

---

1 My roommate and I used *Odds & Evens* to determine who got the bigger bedroom when we moved in together after college. I chose even and won 20 extra square feet.

254. Look for the Return

Apply *Pareto's Principle*[1] to the options and determine which solution gives you the most return for the least amount of effort.

255. Go Pro / Go Con

Create a pros and cons list for your top 5 ideas. Make sure you have at least 5 pros and 5 cons for each (even if they are outlandish[2]).

256. Do the Splits

Try Split Testing if possible. Poll your users or use Google AdWords to try out different ideas or solutions and see which one gets the most traction.

257. Tree-Define It

Make a decision tree of the possible options and follow the one with the most identified benefits.

---

1 *Pareto's Principle* states that 80% of outputs come from 20% of inputs.
2 One "con" of buying this book might be that you become so successful you're made the CEO of your company, which means you'll probably have to move offices.

258. Wheel in the Future

Create a Futures Wheel for each idea.

To do so, pick a possible solution and write it in the center of a piece of paper. List possible direct results/consequences of the solution around the center idea. List possible indirect results/consequences based on the direct results/consequences.

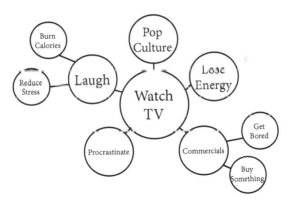

259. Do Nothing

Compare all of your possible solutions to the one option that's always available: Do Nothing.

There's always work that could be done, but given bigger priorities, limited resources, or purely for your own sanity, sometimes you shouldn't do a project.

"Do Nothing" may not be the best solution for an individual project[1], but sometimes it might be the best solution for you, your team, and your company.

---

1 Sometimes "Do Nothing" still is the best option. In the original version of the game *Space Invaders*, the designer discovered that, due to hardware limitations, the level got faster as you killed more aliens. This wasn't intentional, but rather than try to "fix" the problem, he left it in as a way of making the game more challenging. AKA he did nothing. See *Space Invaders*.

260. Follow Precedent

Review previous projects led by you and coworkers that yielded great results and try to follow in their footsteps.

261. Pick the Worst

Try to think of the "worst" decision possible. Write down what makes it so bad and what you definitely want to avoid.

262. Celebrate Rejection

Turn rejecting ideas into a celebration of the idea being turned down. After all, you're one step closer to the right solution.[1]

263. Gain then Lose

Combine your top three ideas into one monster idea[2]. Trim away the excess fat from each idea till you have one awesome (and skinny) solution.

---

1 As Thomas Edison supposedly* said "I have not failed. I've just found 10,000 ways that won't work." *There is some dispute as to whether he actually said this.
2 After all, the incredible color of orange doesn't come from one "idea" itself, it comes from the combination of red and yellow.

264. Go with the Gut

Trust your instincts and make a "gut decision." Revisit the decision the next day and see if it feels right. If it does, keep going with it.

Studies have found that people who trusted their emotions were better at predicting future events than those who didn't place trust in their emotions[1].

Malcolm Gladwell also addresses this phenomenon in his book *Blink*[2]. After researching case studies in both the military and hospitals (places where decisions may mean the difference between life and death), Gladwell concluded:

"We take it, as a given, that the more information decision makers have, the better off they are… All that extra information isn't actually an advantage at all; in fact, you need to know very little to find the underlying signature of a complex phenomenon."[3]

So, just pick something already!

---

1 See *Feelings and Predictions*.
2 See *Blink*.
3 See *Snap Decisions*.

IMPLEMENTATION

*"If there was a problem, yo I'll solve it.
Check out the hook while my DJ revolves it."*
- Vanilla Ice

The most critical phase of problem solving is the implementation of a solution—the actual solving of the problem. Without implementation, nothing is ever actually accomplished[1].

Humor can help make the transition into and out of the implementation phase more effective, as well as keep you and your team engaged and excited about the project.

---

1 You can find additional ideas on implementation in the next chapter on Productivity. This section focuses on those specific to solving a problem.

265. Spin the Bottle

Play spin the bottle in your status meetings. Whoever the bottle lands on has to present the status report or take the meeting minutes.

Other Childhood Games you can alter for implementation[1]:

- Kick the Plan (and Update It With a New One).
- Red Rover, Red Rover, Bring the Memo Over.
- Pillow Forts and Gate Reviews.
- Hide–And–Scope–Creep.
- Tether–Phone.

---

1 For more, or for a list of "rules," check out htww.co/kidgames.

266. Go Away

Take a break between deciding on the solution and starting the implementation. Imagine you're seeing the situation for the first time. Watch a classic "forgotten identity" film like *Bourne Identity* to get into the right mindset.

267. Create a Bat Signal

If delegating the solution to someone else, create the equivalent of a "Bat Signal" for them to use if they need your help[1].

268. Mock Your Solution

Create a mock-up before building the actual solution. Have fun with any placeholders you use. If you have a mock-up that includes a logo that has yet to be designed, use the logo of your favorite candy or sports team until your logo is completed.

269. Show Model Behavior

Build a model of your solution before fully implementing it. Have it walk a "runway" to show it off.

---

1 It could be as simple as a set email header or as cool as lighted sign.

270. Represent Progress

Create a physical representation of the progress of the project. Update it at the end of each day.[1]

271. Bank the Budget

Use Monopoly money to physically represent your budget. Remove it from your piggybank as you use it in the project.[2]

272. Scope Out Limbs

Draw a mascot for the project. Add a new limb each time there's an increase in scope. Remind the project board that with every increase in scope, you're closer to creating a monster.

273. Get Testy

Test after every new addition to the solution. Include small personal details in each test report, such as what you ate prior to testing (just to make sure it didn't skew results).

---

1 E.g. a paper thermometer, a horse race mural, or a money machine with cash in it.
2 If there's any Monopoly money leftover after the project, make it rain.

274. Give Your Version

Have fun with your version terminology. Instead of just numbers, give them codenames, like Google did with their phone OS, Android.

Google's Android Operating System uses a unique naming convention, can you guess what it is?[1]

- Android 1.5 Cupcake
- Android 1.6 Donut
- Android 2.0 Eclair
- Android 2.2 Froyo
- Android 2.3 Gingerbread
- Android 3.0 Honeycomb
- Android 4.0 Ice Cream Sandwich
- Android 4.1 Jelly Bean

---

1 Desserts that start with the next letter in the alphabet.

275. Hide Some Easter Eggs

Have fun with the solution and include an "easter egg" (aka undocumented, hidden features) in the final product.

Some classic easter eggs[1] include:

- On the **Original iPod**: *Select About* from the main menu and then *hold the center button for a few seconds* to launch a mini version of the game *Breakout*.
- In **Mac OS X**: *Type cat /usr/share/calendar/calendar.lotr* into a Terminal window to display important dates from Lord of the Rings.
- In **Skype**: *Type [drunk] or [ninja]* to see some hidden emoticons.
- In **Google Earth**: *Hit Ctrl+Alt+A (Cmd+Alt+A on Mac)* to launch a flight simulator.
- In **Mozilla Firefox**: *Type about:mozilla* into the address bar and you'll see a quote from the Book of Mozilla.

---

1 The term easter egg for this type of hidden feature was coined by *Atari* after the programmer of the game *Adventure* left a secret message in the game. The message? "Created by Warren Robinett."

276. Be Frankenstein

When the final product is ready to launch, hold a "mad scientist" ceremony where you "turn on the switch."

277. Record a Captain's Log

Keep a "Captain's Log" throughout the implementation on how you feel about it and what has and hasn't worked[1].

278. Leave a Mark

Leave your own personal mark on a project with your name or initials hidden somewhere in the solution.

279. Collect Autographs

If getting sign-off from a sponsor or board, have them sign-off in an "autograph book." Include the autographs of the people who worked on it as well.

---

1 Captain's log, stardate 66265.8, I'm finally updating text that said "INSERT ACTUAL STARDATE HERE" with the actual stardate.

280. Give It Away

When the project is over and you are transferring it to another owner, hold a ceremony to "give it away" (like a father with a bride). Crying is optional.

Dearly beloved, we are gathered here today to join together this project with this new project manager.

Do you, project manager, take this project, to own and support from this day forward, for better, for worse, for richer, for poorer, in scope and out of scope, to love and to cherish, till project closure do you part?

[I do.]

And now, by the power invested in me by COMPANY NAME, I hereby pronounce you successfully transistioned. You may now kiss your free-time goodbye.

EVALUATION

"You can observe a lot by watching."
- Yogi Berra

The evaluation phase of problem solving is often overlooked, but is an important step if you want to improve long–term problem solving skills. By tracking how things went, you can prevent "re–inventing the wheel" with every project because you'll know what did or didn't work. Additionally, you can determine if you need another evolution of the solution to take it to the next level.

Humor can be a great way to recap your project, identify new opportunities, and record things to do (or not do) for future projects.

281. Review History

Write the compelling history of how your product came to be. Include interesting trivia.

For inspiration, here are some interesting facts about a few well-known products[1]:

- **WD-40** was born when 3 rocket scientists tried to develop a substance that would prevent corrosion in rockets by displacing water. They got it to work on their 40th try, and thus named the substance "Water Displacement—40th Try" or WD-40.
- **Penicillin** was discovered by accident. Dr. Alexander Fleming was growing staphylococci cultures in his lab when he decided to take a vacation. He failed to clean out his petri dish and, when he came back two weeks later, noticed one dish covered in mold and all the bacteria dead.
- **Popsicle**[2] had its start when 11-year-old Frank Epperson accidentally left a stick in his soft drink overnight and discovered the soda frozen to the stick. 18 years later he patented the idea and started selling it.

---

1 See *Unique Origins.*
2 Popsicle is a proprietary eponym, or a brand name that has come into general use for the entire class of products. Other examples include: Kleenex, Band-Aid, Hula Hoop, Ping Pong, and Super Glue. See *Proprietary Eponyms.*

282. Picture the Process

Take pictures during the course of the project and create a slideshow or video once it's all over.

283. Sound Off

Find a song that encapsulates the overall feeling of the project after it's been completed. Play it during your final presentation.[1]

284. Statistically Speak

Calculate interesting statistics for your project, such as: number of emails sent, meetings held, scope changes, and versions [2]

285. Draw a Tree

Draw a tree. Label the roots as the problem, the trunk as solutions and the leaves as results.

---

1 *We Are the Champions*, *Chariots of Fire* and *Since You've Been Gone* are favorites.
2 To see statistics about this book, visit htww.co/bookstats.

286. Map the Mind

Draw a mind map of the solution and any future next steps.[1]

287. Go Back to Your Day

Review how your solution has improved things by comparing things from "back in your day" to how they are today.

288. Travel through Time

Think about how people through time would see your solution. How would they view the results 5, 10, 50, or 1,000 years ago? What about 5, 10, 50, or 1,000 years in the future?

289. SWOT the Idea

Analyze your solution using a SWOT analysis: identify Strengths, Weaknesses, Opportunities, and Threats. Capture notes for future improvements or new projects.[2]

---

1 Find out more about mind mapping at htww.co/mindmap.
2 Wearing SWAT gear like body armor and helmets is optional but loads of fun.

290. Apply McLuhan

Answer Marshall McLuhan's tetrad of questions[1] in context of your solution:

1. "What does it enhance?"
2. "What does it make obsolete?"
3. "What does it bring back that was once obsolete?"
4. "What does it turn into when taken to the extreme?"

An example: *Solving my hunger by getting a milkshake.*

1. My taste buds with deliciousness.
2. My desire for food.
3. Nostalgia of other milkshakes. A smile to my face.
4. I get all sustenance from liquid form. The world runs out of milk. I lose lactose intolerant readers.

---

1 McLuhan used these questions to better understand the effects different types of technology and mediums had on society. See *McLuhan*. I learned them from Jeff Michalski, founder of *Second City ETC* and renowned improv teacher. He used them to develop satire based on the news.

291. Find the Funny

Write (or hire someone to write) a stand-up set about your final product. Use the "truth in comedy" to explore the idea further.

Comedian and marketing consultant Rajiv Satyal does this through his program *Funny 'Cause It's True*. The program "uses comedians to uncover compelling consumer truths that makes your brand's advertising and communication resonate more strongly with your target market."

In essence, they hire comedians to write material about your product, and then review the funniest bits and get at the heart of why they are funny and what that means about your solution.

And, it's worked for brands like *Gillette*, *Herbal Essences*, and *Dannon*.[1]

---

1 Find out more at www.standpointagency.com.

292. Blackout

Try to find out what could be removed from your solution by strategically blacking out words in your project closure report.[1]

293. Check the Checks

Evaluate how each phase of the process went, even evaluating the evaluation process.

294. Take Suggestions

Have a suggestion box to allow continual feedback from users. Also mention that people can submit positive feedback.

295. Survey Success

Survey the stakeholders of the solution. In addition to basic questions, include questions on things like logo, team name, and favorite project moment.

---

1 Austin Kleon did just that in his book, *Newspaper Blackout*, described as "a book of poetry made by redacting newspaper articles with a permanent marker." Find out more at htww.co/blackout.

296. Move Forward with Feedback

Survey your team for at least one thing they liked about your contribution to the project and one thing you could improve.

297. Remix It

Imagine you were going to "remix" your project. What elements would you definitely keep (or "sample" for future projects) and what would you remove?[1]

298. Pick On Yourself

Add the project results to your resume picklist—a document you keep of your accomplishments for annual reviews and updating your resume[2]. Include one fun detail.

299. Stump the Issue

Pretend you are running for President of the United States. What would critics and supporters say about your project "record?"

---

1 Get inspired by some of the best remixes of all time at htww.co/remix.
2 You do have an "accomplishments picklist" right?

300. Do It Again

Give at least 5 things you would do differently if you had to do it all over again, 5 things you would do the same, and 5 ways you could have had more fun with the project.

5 Ways I Could Have Had More Fun Writing This Book[1]:

1. Solicited more ideas from readers and clients (because I like learning new ways too).
2. Worked with another person to share the responsibility of doing all the research.
3. Sent copies out for feedback sooner. Some of the edits have been hilarious.
4. Told people about the book earlier (I love talking to people about it).
5. Included more puns.

---

1 To be clear, I already had a ton of fun writing the book, but there's always room for improvement.

SKILL #4:
PRODUCTIVITY

All the communicating, relationship–building, and problem solving in the world do you little good if you never actually execute the plan, do the work, and get things done. Humor can help increase productivity for yourself and for others.

Productivity is about time, energy, and skill management. It means managing your time so you can actually get work finished, having the energy and motivation to actually do the work when that time comes, and possessing the necessary skill to complete the work sufficiently.

In today's world almost everyone is busy (aka they "do things"). Good workers are efficient (they "do things right"). Great workers are effective (they "do the right things"). The best workers are efficient and effective (they "do the right things the right way").

Productivity and the Letter "P"

The letter "p" is surprisingly important when it comes to productivity. First, it is in fact called **p**roductivity–the ability to produce.

Second, smart businesses follow **P**areto's **P**rinciple to know what to produce and for whom. They focus on the 20% of customers/issues/employees that lead to 80% of the sales/lack of sales/results/lack of results.

Third, productivity and actually completing the work often adheres to **P**arkinson's Law, which states "work expands so as to fill the time available for its completion."[1]

Fourth, productive employees use systems like the **P**omodoro Technique (see #311) which creates micro-deadlines (helping you avoid Parkinson's Law) and gives time for Strategic Disengagement (see the next chapter).

Finally, people who follow these principles become successful **p**residents (CEOs), **p**oster children for success, and "**p**ersons, very important."

And, naturally, humor can help every step of the **p**way.[2]

---

1 Basically if you give yourself a week to do something, it'll likely take a week (and often you won't really work on it till right before it's due, aka **p**rocrastination). See *Parkinson's Law*.
2 The "p" is silent.

Humor and Productivity

Humor can go a long way in improving workplace efficiency and effectiveness. Various studies have shown humor can increase productivity and, when used appropriately, does not detract from tasks requiring increased concentration[1].

For this book, we're going to think about productivity in the way we do our work, as defined below:

- **Planning** – Knowing what to work on and when to do it (including Time Management).
- **Motivation** – Having the motivation, energy, and focus to actually work on the task at hand (including Energy Management).
- **Skill Building** – Ensuring you have the skills to do the task.
- **Fun For Yourself** – Improving your own productivity by adding some fun to your work, just for you.
- **Fun For Others** – Improving other people's productivity (and your own effectiveness) by adding some fun to your work and others'.

With these ways in mind, here are 100 ways to use humor to increase productivity.

---

1 See *Humor and Performance*.

PLANNING

"The main thing is to keep the main thing the main thing."
- Stephen R. Covey

Knowing what to work on is critical to successful execution; it doesn't matter how efficient you are if you're not working on the right thing. Planning and managing your time helps ensure you'll always be focused on the right thing and will have time to actually work on it.

Humor can help you find creative ways of creating your plan and scheduling time to actually execute it.

301. Enter the Matrix

Learn the Eisenhower matrix (made popular by Stephen R. Covey). Classify tasks based on each Quadrant and work on those in Q1 and Q2.

	Urgent	Not Urgent
Important	Big Deadline Crying Baby Desk Fire Q1	Exercise Training Humor Q2
Not Important	Q3 Emails Distractions Interruptions	Q4 Gossip Busy Work Mindlessness

Q1. Urgent & Important. Do these immediately.
Q2. Not Urgent, Important. Schedule these on your calendar.
Q3. Urgent, Not Important. Delegate these if possible[1].
<u>**Q4.** Not Urgent,</u> Not Important. Eliminate these[2].

1 Delegation is not always possible, just make sure you don't sacrifice items in Q1 and Q2 for Q3. And yes, email falls here. If something is truly urgent and important, people will call you or stop by your desk.
2 Recreation is Q2, not Q4. See the next chapter on *Strategic Disengagement*.

302. Find the Perpetrator

Meticulously track your days for a week. Pretend you are a CSI analyst trying to find ways to be more efficient.[1]

303. Review Your Day

Before going to sleep, mentally go through your day and evaluate how it went. For added fun, try doing it as a sportscaster.

304. Address Yourself

Write a letter to yourself describing where you want to be after the next 3, 6, and/or 12 months; include a joke.

305. Give Tasks a Hand

Each week, think of five tasks you'd like to accomplish that week. Assign them to digits on your hand: thumb is for your most important project, index is for something for a long–term goal, middle finger is something just for you, ring finger is something for someone else, pinky is miscellaneous.

---

1 When I first did this, I learned a lot about myself. I found out I'm most productive between 1pm and 8pm, so in a way, it's a "crime" to my productivity to be up early.

306. Flowchart Decisions

Create a flowchart of decisions you have to make more than once. How does this improve productivity?

Peter Drucker says "an executive who makes many decisions is both lazy and ineffectual."[1] This comes from the idea that, where possible, an effective person creates systems, processes, and rules to guide their behavior, rather than make new decisions each day.

After all, you don't decide a new order of getting dressed every morning. It's underwear then pants, every day[2].

To demonstrate, here's a flowchart I follow every day:

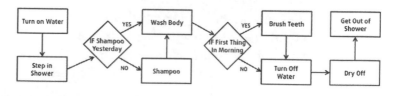

---

1 See *The Effective Executive*.
2 Unless you're Superman.

307. Go to BATL

Create a BATL[1] Plan. It captures everything you COULD do. *Every* task. Review it weekly and promote tasks that should be accomplished that week.

308. Don't Do Something

Create a TO DON'T List—a list of things you could do, but achieving them would not be effective or strategic.

309. Cut Your Losses

Stop doing projects not aligned with your long-term goals. Get over the aversion to sunk costs by celebrating the time, resource, and happiness savings you'll get when you decide to kill a project.

310. Break It Down

Break down your project into 5 steps. Break each step into 5 actionable tasks. Break each task into 5 actions (make sure one of the actions is something you enjoy doing).[2]

1 It stands for Big A** Task-List.
2 In Project Management, this is known as a Work Breakdown Structure, because if you don't do it, the project manager has a breakdown.

311. Tomato Your Time

Follow the Pomodoro Technique: get a timer and work in periods of 25 minutes, followed by a break of 5 minutes.

Using a structured timetable like this helps improve planning, enhance focus, and maintain motivation—all while ensuring you still get work done and take a break every once in a while.

Some helpful tips from www.pomodorotechnique.com[1]:

- Once the Pomodoro (the 25–minute work increment) starts, keep working until the timer goes off.
- If a task takes less than one Pomodoro, start working on the next task.
- After 4 or 5 Pomodoros, take a longer break of at least 20–30 minutes.
- Experiment to find the best intervals for you. Maybe it's 25/5, or it could be 50/10 or 75/15.

---

1 Definitely check out the website where you'll find resources on how to get started, why it works, and more, all for free.

312. Schedule the Details

Schedule a "productivity day" where you plan out, by the minute, your day.

I don't recommend doing this every day (the average workday is filled with meetings and interruptions), but it can be great for when you have a big deadline coming up.

Here's an example Productivity Day I used for this book[1].

00:30-08:00 — Sleep (exactly 7.5 hours).
08:00-08:10 — Wake up. Drink water. Stretch.
08:10-09:00 — Answer emails. Drink orange juice.
09:00-09:30 — Plan upcoming tasks. Eat breakfast (*Rice Krispies*).
09:30-10:45 — Edit *Planning* section. Drink water.
10:45-11:00 — Mental break. Bio break.
11:00-12:15 — Edit *Motivation* section. Drink water.
12:15-12:30 — Mental break. Eat snack (Celery with peanut butter).
12:30-13:45 — Edit *Skill Building* section. Drink water.
13:45-14:15 — Eat lunch (chicken nugget salad). Write pun-filled tweet.
14:15-15:30 — Edit *Fun For You* section. Drink water.
15:30-16:00 — Mental break. Bio break. Check email.
16:00-17:15 — Edit *Fun For Others* section. Drink water.
17:15-18:15 — Exercise (run 3 miles). Shower. Eat snack (carrots).
18:15-19:00 — Answer email. Drink *Gatorade*.
19:00-20:00 — Eat dinner (*Skyline Chili* dip). Watch *The Daily Show*.
20:00-00:00 — IMPROV!
00:00-00:30 — Check *ESPN* / *Facebook* / *reddit*.

---

1 I did almost this exact schedule (with the meals and evening activities changing) for a week to finish round three of edits for the entire book.

313. Meet with a "Friend"

Name your computer. Schedule meetings with that name to block off time to get work done.[1]

314. Isolate Yourself

Schedule a half–day of *No Distractions*. Block off your calendar (see #313), turn on out–of–office notifications and work from a place where people can't distract you.

315. Schedule Discussion

Schedule a half–day of *Unstructured Discussions*. Make it a point to walk around and casually talk with others about what they are working on and how things are going for them (both personal and work–related). Combine with #314.

316. Go to the Bank

Set up a "bank account" of time for meetings each week. Once it's depleted, tell people to schedule meetings for next week.[2]

---

1 This book was primarily written on a Mac Pro named MacKenzie.
2 This is particularly great for managers of others. Work with your team to agree on the overall bank account size, withdrawal limits for each person, and overdraft fees.

MOTIVATION

"People often say that motivation doesn't last. Well, neither does bathing—that's why we recommend it daily."
- Zig Ziglar

Unfortunately, just because something is on your calendar, it doesn't necessarily mean you're going to want to do it. Instead, procrastination creeps in and you'd do just about anything to avoid actually executing. Motivation is needed to get you to not only work, but to work on the right things.

Humor can be an expert motivator, providing a boost in energy or change in mindset that transforms "I don't wanna!" into "Let's do this!"

317. Provide Some Background

Change your desktop background to something motivational
(such as a picture of your family or your favorite vacation spot)[1].

318. Be Inspired

Start off each day by watching an inspirational video. Just type
"inspiration" into Google, YouTube or Humor's Office[2].

319. Motivate

Find a motivational poster and hang it in your cubicle or use it as
a mousepad[3].

320. Laugh-tivate

#319 not your style? Get a de-motivational poster[4].

---

1 Get started with desktop backgrounds at htww.co/backgrounds.
2 Check it out at www.humorsoffice.com.
3 Find great posters at htww.co/motivate.
4 Find just as great posters at htww.co/demotivate.

321. Lock–in Inspiration

Create easy–to–remember, hard–to–hack, inspirational passwords.

To do so, simply think of a sentence that inspires or motivates you (or makes you laugh), and then use the first letter of each word as your password. It's easy to remember (just say the sentence in your head), but hard to crack (since it doesn't contain actual words).

To further improve security, substitute numbers and symbols for letters when possible.

Here are a few of my old passwords[1]:

> DDw2cDrs = *Did Drew write 2day cuz Drew really should.*
> Qsascfs2 = *Quit snoozin and start creating fun stuff 2do.*
> Swwswas3 = *Soon we will stop working and start 3njoying.*
> Taj2dhhh = *Tell A Joke 2Day. Ha Ha Ha.*
> Wi6ao7b789 = *Why Is 6 Afraid of 7? Because 7 8 9.*

---

1 Note to the hackers: none of these are my current password for anything. Except maybe my MySpace page.

322. Trigger Motivation

Create a list of all the things that motivate you and demotivate you. When you need to get something done, do something on the motivate list (while avoiding things on the demotivate list).

Here's a list for me:

MOTIVATORS

Accomplishing a goal.

Reading a business book.

Catching up with friends.

Listening to upbeat music.

Reviewing previous accolades.

DEMOTIVATORS

Talking to negative people.

The *Buckeyes* losing[1].

Not having any fun.

Hitting snooze.

Feeling sick.

---

1 Yes, I realize it seems kind of silly that my motivation is tied to the sports teams of *The Ohio State University*, but it's true. I realize now that if I want to be productive on the day the *Buckeyes* play, I better get everything done before I watch the game or look at the score.

323. Pump It Up

Get energized for the day by listening to some of your favorite songs on your commute to work[1].

324. Picture the Good Stuff

Get a digital picture frame and fill it with pictures of your friends, family, pets, and material objects that make you happy.

325. Find Your Tribe

Find a community of people doing what you want to do. Do a Google search or check out Meetup.com for communities.

326. Go Long

Have a list of your long-term goals posted at your desk. Before starting any project, remind yourself of how it links to what you ultimately want to accomplish[2].

---

1 I'm a big fan of the DJ *Girl Talk*. He remixes old and new songs together for high-beats-per-minute awesomeness. Warning: many of the songs are explicit. And catchy.
2 Did you know that people who list out their goals are 10 times more likely to actually achieve them? See *Statistics on New Year's Resolutions*.

327. Game Your Productivity

Turn your productivity into a game using gamification[1]: use an app like *EpicWin* to track stats, level up, and earn rewards for being productive.

328. Think Accomplishments

While working on tasks you hate, think of how much you've accomplished, not how much you have left. "Wow, I'm already 3% through this report."

329. Finish Them

Concentrate on completing tasks, not just starting them. Reward yourself when you complete a task, even if it's just a fist pump.

330. Eat the Frog

Do the hardest / least pleasing thing on your task list first thing in the morning. Everything after that will seem easier.[2]

---

1 Gamification refers to the integration of game elements into systems and processes. Learn more at htww.co/gamify.
2 "Eat a live frog first thing in the morning and nothing worse will happen to you the rest of the day." - Mark Twain

331. Do the Minimum

If you don't feel like doing something, at least do the smallest amount of noticeable work before moving to something else.

Oftentimes starting is enough to motivate you to continue, but even if you don't keep on going, at least you've done something.

A few examples:

- **Working out:** At least put on your workout shoes and do one rep of one exercise.
- **Eating Healthier:** Eat one piece of a vegetable before eating anything else.[1]
- **Quitting smoking:** Throw out one cigarette for each one you smoke.
- **Writing a book / project update / dissertation[2]:** Write at least one sentence a day.

---

1 I have to do this otherwise I'd eat exclusively like an 8 year old.
2 If you are my brother, or someone else who is ABD (All But Dissertation), seriously, get to work on it! You're almost finished with your PhD!

332. Hack Writer's Block

If you have writer's block, just start typing like you're a hacker in a movie (randomly hitting keys as fast as you can). Gradually let it turn into real words and then into sentences related to what you want to write about.

333. Be Arbitrary

While working, set arbitrary goals to reach. Such as, when going through email choose your favorite number between 1 and 25 and try to keep your number of unread emails to less than or equal to that number[1].

334. Auto-Archive

Set a filter to automatically archive email older than a day or two. The knowledge they will "disappear" promotes a quick response.

335. Stand-up for Meetings

Having "standing only" meetings (no one's allowed to sit).[2]

---

1 I try to hit 5, 8, 12, or 24 emails.
2 Want even shorter meetings? Have "dancing only" meetings.

336. Create a Bio Deadline

Decide on a task to complete. Sit down and don't move from your spot until you complete the task, not even to use the restroom. You'll start working faster once you realize you need a bio break. To increase the sense of urgency, drink water while working.[1]

337. Unplug Yourself

Unplug your laptop. Stop working when the battery is drained.

338. Show Your Status

Create physical status messages for your desk. Use both "away messages" and colors for Available, Busy, and Do Not Disturb.

339. Prevent Distractions

Create a list of things that distract you. Think of ways to prevent those distractions[2].

---

1 Speaking of which, I better wrap up this section soon...
2 One study showed the average employee is interrupted every 15 minutes and that it can take up to 20 minutes to get back on task afterwards. See *Coping with Distractions*.

340. Procrastinate Productively

Have a procrastination to-do list: a list of easy-to-do things for when you aren't motivated to do the tasks on your to-do list.

While you'll still be procrastinating, at least you'll be doing it in a somewhat productive manner.

A few items on my procrastination to-do list:

- Watch a TED talk (www.ted.com).
- Search Google for industry news.
- Read articles I've marked as "Read Later."
- Send a Thank You card or email.
- Straighten up my desk (or my office (or my room)).
- Update my list of *Movies I've Seen* or *Places I've Been*.
- Compose and tweet a pun.

SKILL BUILDING

"The depressing thing about tennis is that no matter how good I get, I'll never be as good as a wall."
- Mitch Hedburg

Assuming you have the plan, the time, and the motivation, the last step is making sure you've got the skill. Making an effort to "sharpen the saw" up–front can save you time on the back–end by improving efficiency and skill.

Humor can sharpen with the best of them, helping you enjoy skill building and using what you learn.

341. Qualify Quality Days

Create a list of five things you'd like to do every day. If you do at least three of them, consider it a Quality Day. If you do all five, mark it as a Perfect Day.

Keep track of the results and review monthly. Make changes based on what you do easily and what is harder.

One crucial mindset to have[1]: the goal is Quality Days, *not* Perfect Days. Your list of 5 should be so challenging that it's difficult to get a Perfect Day, but manageable to achieve 3 of 5.

My five goals from 2011. (Total # of Quality Days: 364)

1. Don't hit snooze.   (Days Completed: 232)
2. Do one *Humor That Works* task.   (Days Completed: 322)
3. Do at least 20 minutes of Exercise.   (Days Completed: 274)
4. Eat at least 2 fruits or vegetables.   (Days Completed: 323)
5. Do something solely for fun.   (Days Completed: 363)

---

1 In 2010, I had a goal of not hitting snooze. Sadly, I failed that goal, a lot. What's worse was any day I hit snooze, I lost motivation for the rest of the day ("well, I already failed my goal for the day, why do anything else"). In 2011, I came up with Quality Days. If I had 5 goals to shoot for, but only hit 3, I'd still consider it a success. So even if I hit snooze in the morning, there were 4 other habits I could do and still feel like I had a good day. This one change has led to the biggest improvement in me establishing new habits.

342. Work It Out

Create a workout plan for a softskill you want to learn, such as doing five reps of reading a sentence out loud for getting better at public speaking.

343. Limit Your Sentence

Improve your brevity of writing by putting a word or sentence limit on email responses.[1]

344. Set a Record

Time yourself on repetitive tasks. Try to beat your fastest time while still doing everything correctly. Keep a "fastest time" scoresheet at your desk

345. Put a Birdie on Your Shoulder

Show someone else how you normally do something. Ask for their feedback on ways to do it more effectively.[2]

---

1 Check out three.sentenc.es.
2 My personal preference is to ask them to start any tips with "I say, I say ..." like Foghorn Leghorn.

346. Be a Shadow

Shadow a peer, manager, direct report, or customer for an hour or a day. Write down what you learn.

347. Be a Teacher

Teach someone else a skill that you would like to be an expert in.[1] Ask them what they've learned from you.

348. Listen Up

Listen to a podcast or audiobook talking about a skill you use everyday.[2]

349. Excerpt an Expert

Read a page from *Getting Things Done* or another productivity book, even if you've read it before.

---

1 Studies show that when you teach someone else, you work harder to understand the material, recall it more accurately, and apply it more effectively. See *The Protégé Effect*.
2 Check out htww.co/podcasts for some recommendations.

350. Answer to Drucker

In *The Effective Executive*, Peter Drucker lists what an effective executive should know about his or her own productivity.[1] I've turned those ideas into a list of productivity questions, plus added a few of my own.

Answer these questions about your own working style:

- *Do you work better in the morning or at night?*
- *Do you need to make a number of drafts fast (rapid prototyping) or work meticulously on one draft?*
- *Are you more productive on a team or by yourself?*
- *Do you prefer having a detailed outline or would you rather just get started?*
- *Do you perform better when you have plenty of time or with deadlines looming?*
- *Do you learn better by reading a document or listening to someone talk about a subject?*
- *What posture makes you the most productive?*
- *How long can you be productive before needing a break (25 minutes, 50 minutes, 75 minutes)?*
- *What type of breaks help you maintain productivity (exercise, humor, thinking, napping)?*

---

1 See *The Effective Executive*.

351. Take a Shortcut

Print out a list of shortcuts for a program or operating system you use frequently. Force yourself to learn them by disconnecting your mouse and only using your keyboard.

List of helpful shortcuts (for Windows & Mac):

Shortcut	Windows	Mac
OPERATING SYSTEM		
Task Manager	Ctrl+Alt+Del	Opt+Cmd+Esc
Switch Applications	Ctrl+Tab	Cmd+Tab
Launch Shortcut	Windows+R	Cmd+Space
MOST APPLICATIONS		
Select All	Ctrl+A	Cmd+A
Cut Selected	Ctrl+X	Cmd+X
Copy Selected	Ctrl+C	Cmd+C
Paste Selected	Ctrl+V	Cmd+V
Find Something	Ctrl+F	Cmd+F
MOST WEB BROWSERS		
Go to Address Bar	Ctrl+L	Cmd+L
Add "www." and ".com"	Ctrl+Enter	Cmd+Enter
Create New Tab	Ctrl+T	Cmd+T
Reopen Closed Tab	Ctrl+Shift+T	Cmd+Shift+T

352. Learn from the "Best"

Search YouTube for "Best way to [INSERT SKILL HERE]" You can find tutorials on topics ranging from folding a fitted sheet to keeping a bag of chips fresh without a chip clip.[1]

353. Confer with Experts

Attend a conference specific to your industry or work. Register with an awesome nickname like "Drudacris" or "Pip."

354. Class It Up

Take a continuing education course at a local university in something you care about.[2]

355. Add an Acronym

Add an acronym to the end of your name by getting certified in a field related to your work. Have a "graduation" party when you receive your certification.[3]

---

1 Check out htww.co/kingtuts for some of my favorite tutorials.
2 It's amazing how different school is when you're there because you choose to be.
3 Possible certifications to look into: PhD, PMP, CSP, CPA, PHP, BRB, LOL, 007.

356. Resume Humor

Include sense of humor on your resume. Look for it on people's resumes when you're hiring.

Note: *This may be the most controversial tip in the entire book. Proceed with caution and decide what's best for you.*

I've read a number of articles on "resume tips" and most will tell you NOT to include humor. Here's my take:

1. First, many of these posts saying NOT to do it talk about "jokes." You already know adding humor to your resume doesn't mean being a comedian. Instead, you're using it for amusement, such as just listing "sense of humor" as a skill.
2. If you're looking to fill a job and you want a candidate you can relate to, why not list sense of humor as a quality you're looking for?[1]
3. If you're looking for a job and humor is a skill you possess, why wouldn't you include it, along with other soft skills like public speaking or technical skills like proficiency at PHP?
4. Finally, if a place won't hire you, or a candidate won't work for you, because you listed "sense of humor," are they really a good fit?

1 I know of more than a few people who included "sense of humor" on job posts and were happy with the results, including the mayor of a major city.

FUN FOR YOU

"Whatever is fun, do it more."
- Jill Bernard

Not everything you do is going to be I–wish–I–could–do–this–everyday fun, but it can be this–doesn't–suck–as–bad fun. Not only will it help you do the task better, you'll also be happier. It's also something other people can't take away from you.[1]

Being effective while having fun is what humor is all about. It also helps put your personal signature on the work you do, separating it from the work of other people around you.

---

1 Some people work for tyrannical bosses who put the kibosh on any inkling of fun. This section is for those unfortunate souls (and everyone else). These examples of humor only impact you and can't be controlled by an ineffective manager.

357. Slink Along

Get a slinky; play with it quietly while talking on conference calls.

358. Pack a Sack

If you pack a lunch, bring it in a themed lunch pail like when you were in elementary school.[1]

359. Style a Reputation

Develop your own style within the guidelines of your company's dress code. For me it's solid–color, bright shirts from *Express*. Someone else in my office had a great collection of blazers.

360. Supply Office Humor

If you get your own office supplies, have fun with them. Get a pen with a customized photo, a Swingline Red Stapler (a la *Office Space*), or a cool tape dispenser.[2]

---

1 If a lunch pail isn't your thing, turn your sack lunch into art: htww.co/paperbag.
2 Check out thinkgeek.com for a collection of cool "geek" products.

361. Sit Like a King

Order the best, most comfortable chair you can. Make sure you set it up to be ergonomically correct.[1]

Tips for sitting more comfortably from the Mayo Clinic[2]:

- Sit with your back straight and your thighs horizontal (making a 90 degree angle).
- Adjust your chair so your feet rest comfortably on the floor and your knees are level with your hips.
- Adjust the monitor height so the top is even with or slightly below eye level. Position it arm's length away.
- When typing, avoid bending your wrists up and down and keep them in a straight, natural position.

If you can't achieve the above with your current desk, tell your manager you need to change. If the fact that it's a medical issue doesn't help, cite it as a profit / loss issue.[3]

1 Hat tip to Palmo Carpino for the reminder on the importance of our seats. Palmo is "Second Fiddle, First Class, Third String Humour Resultant" at *from Pen to Platform*. Find out more at www.palmocarpino.com.
2 See *Office Ergonomics*.
3 According the CDC, Work–related musculoskeletal disorders (WMSDs) cost American companies ~$50 billion per year in compensation costs, lost wages, and lost productivity. See *WMSD Prevention*.

362. Dictate Your Message

Dictate the text of a document through a peer or a program like *Dragon Naturally–Speaking*.

363. Accent Your Email

When writing an email, write with a British (or other) accent in your head. See if you use different vocabulary. Just don't get too cheeky about it or else people may think you're barmy.

364. Don't Live Edit

Turn off autocorrect and write a first draft without eaditing anyhting (even missspellings). See how good you are at typ**ign**.[1]

365. Register Humor

Use a fun surname or title when registering software.[2]

---

1 Claerly I'm nnot vry goo00000oood.
2 The first draft of this book was written in a copy of Microsoft Word registered to "Winnie the Drew."

366. Be a Character

Do a work task as if you were your favorite character from a movie or comic book. HULK SMASH GRAMMAR ERRORS!

367. Play Favorites

Work things like your favorite color or food into your work.[1]

368. Create a Legend

Add a fictional item to the legend of a graph (that has no impact on the visual) and see if people notice.

369. Use Invisible Ink

Add hidden messages in emails and documents (such as using white font on white background) just for fun.[2]

---

1 A number of my projects include the color orange. Nearly all of my lunch meetings take place at locations that serve milkshakes.
2 You will not *believe* what's written in the blank space above. I can't believe I got away with putting that in a business book!

370. Doodle Your Notes

Capture meeting notes in a mind map or through doodles.[1]
You can also write them in an interesting color or with
crayons.

Below are the visual notes version of the "General Dos" of
using humor, shared on page 8.[2]

---

1 This is known as "visual note–taking." Find out more at htww.co/visualnotes.
2 As you can see, it doesn't require you to be a great artist. Just draw!

371. Listen Closely

Listen to your favorite type of music when working to get a boost in mood and productivity[1].

For me, I listen to different types of music depending on what I'm working on:

Classical — when I really need to concentrate.
Hip Hop — when working on repetitive tasks.
Rock — when doing something physical.
Movie Soundtracks[2] — when writing.
Oldies — when answering emails.
Adele — when I want to sing.

---

1 Studies show listening to music can improve your mood and lower your perception of tension. Contrary to popular belief, however, your personal preference for music is more important than the type of music you listen to. See *Music and Productivity*.
2 Hat tip to David Tarvin (my brother) for suggesting movie soundtracks. He tells his students to listen to them when writing commemorative speeches as it "makes their speeches build and climax like the music."

372. Soundtrack Your Project

Create a soundtrack for your project. It could be as simple as music by a single artist, an album you like, or a custom mix. Play the soundtrack whenever you're working on the project[1].

373. Play a Song

Learn *Mary Had A Little Lamb*[2] on touch tone phones; play it while waiting for a phone conference to start. Better yet, play *Happy Birthday*[3] when it's a coworker's birthday.

374. Sing a Start

Start your day or meeting off by singing your country's national anthem (to yourself or with others).

375. Beat Your Work Up

Establish a rhythm in your head when doing monotonous tasks. Do different actions on "beats" of the rhythm.

---

1 This book's soundtrack included a mix of *21, The Soundtrack to Jurassic Park* and *Frankie Valli — Greatest Hits.*
2 The "notes": 6 5 4 5 6 6 6 5 5 5 6 8 8 / 6 5 4 5 6 6 6 6 5 5 6 5 4.
3 The "notes": 1 1 2 1 6 3 / 1 1 2 1 9 6 / 1 1 # 9 6 3 2 / # # 9 6 9 6.

376. Answer Alphabetically

Find a creative or unique way to do a boring task, such as answering emails in alphabetical order.

377. Invert Your View

Invert the colors of your computer screen.[1]

378. Fill a Notebook

Act like a stand–up comedian and always have pen & paper (or your phone) to capture your ideas and jokes as you have them.[2]

379. Touchdown on Celebrations

Do a touchdown celebration dance when you've successfully accomplished something.[3]

---

1 Some studies suggest this actually helps reduce eye strain as well. Give it a try!
2 I personally use *Evernote*. Check it out at Evernote.com
3 My personal favorite is the Ickey Shuffle. Who Dey!

380. Live Your Dreams

Think back to when you were a kid. What did you dream about being when you grew up? Find ways to incorporate whatever it was into your work now.

Did you want to be a(n)...	Do this...
Action Star	When driving to / from work, pretend you're tailing someone.
Astronaut	Before starting a new activity, countdown to "liftoff."
Doctor	Eat meals as if you were doing surgery on the food.
Magician	Learn magic tricks that can be used to illustrate points.
Rock Star	Write some of your sentences as song lyrics.
Sports Superstar	Before doing a presentation, listen to the *Chicago Bulls* entrance music.

FUN FOR OTHERS

"Laugh and the whole world laughs with you.
Cry and... you have to blow your nose."
- A First Grader's take on the saying

We know that accomplishing tasks in a fun way
can improve productivity, so why not involve your
coworkers. In addition to improving team effectiveness,
you'll also improve the relationships of those involved
and likely increase some workplace satisfaction as well.

Humor in the workplace is all about adding levity and
raising the spirits of those around you.

381. Invite Parties

Send out your meeting invitations as if they were to a rocking party.

Here's an example from a project meeting update:

HAPPY
STATUS DAY!
to PROJECT
X-caliber!

JOIN US ON
MONDAY AUGUST, 23
AT 2:30 PM.
FOR THE CELEBRATION
OF OUR VERY OWN
PROJECT X-CALIBER'S
WEEKLY STATUS UPDATE
THERE WILL BE:
Project Updates,
Upcoming Milestones,
Risk Assessments,
And Actionable Next Steps!

382. Put in the Silly

Get some silly putty to play with at meetings. Hand it out to coworkers as well.

383. Eat Candy

Provide candy at meetings. Get thematic and provide *Smarties* for brainstorming, *Pay Days* for financial meetings, etc.[1]

384. Share Accomplishments

When starting a meeting, have each person share one thing they are proud of (something recent, ideally non–work–related) before starting with the work stuff.

385. Pass Notes

When exchanging information in a meeting, pass a note to a coworker like you did in grade school.[2]

---

1 Naturally, as a comedian who makes people laugh, my favorite candy is a... *Milky Way* (did you think I was going to say *Snickers*?)
2 Psssst... What'd you get for "#17 - What's the status of your project?"

386. Shoot Hoops

As you finish pages of your agenda, encourage everyone to crumple up their paper and try to shoot it into the wastebasket.

387. Dip in the Poll

Use polling features in virtual meeting software. Include at least one or two questions for fun, such as favorite TV show from the 90s or least favorite household chore.[1]

388. Use the Board

Use the "whiteboard" in virtual meetings to get all attendees involved. Test the functionality out by drawing a picture.

389. Take Note

Take meeting minutes—include fun/interesting/random thoughts you have while in the meeting.[2]

---

1 My favorite 90s TV show was *MacGyver*. My least favorite chore is making the bed.
2 I went back through some of my old notes to find an example. Apparently, in a meeting about web development, I thought "shouldn't the trial version of applications be called 'app-etizers?'"

390. Read the Not News

Share a news story from a site like *Fark.com* (not news) or *TheOnion.com* (fake news) at the end of a meeting.

Here are some great headlines from *Fark.com*:

- *Five wildly popular car modifications that must be stopped. SPOILER ALERT*
- *British terror alert status upgraded to "What's all this, then?"*
- *Man wakes up with pants on fire, although police doubt his story.*
- *Two year old refuses to sleep during day, may get charged with resisting a rest.*
- *Man plays electric guitar so loud that neighbor's fish jumps. It must have been a bass guitar.*
- *Full set of teeth successfully grown in lab, scientists awarded with plaque.*

391. Survey with Humor

Include an off the wall question[1] in your next
department– or company–wide survey.

One of my favorites is "How much wood could a
woodchuck chuck if a woodchuck could chuck wood?"

Some popular answers[2] to this very question:

- None. Woodchucks can't actually chuck wood.
- According to a wildlife expert, if they could chuck
  would, it would be around 700 pounds.
- A woodchuck would chuck all the wood he could if a
  woodchuck could chuck wood.

---

1 E.g., which Michael Jackson album was released in 1979?
2 See *How Much Wood.*

392. Teach a Message

Include interesting facts as part of your IM away message.[1]

393. Dial It Up

Try to get a phone number that can spell something memorable. Or lookup the phone number you're calling to see what words it could spell and share it with the person.[2]

394. Have F.U.N.

Name your next project something that has a silly / hidden acronym, such as my Database Utility for Managed Business.[3]

395. Do Some Branding

Create a logo and theme music for one of your projects; use it whenever you do status updates or send out emails.

---

1 For example, did you know that nerve cells create electrical impulses that reach speeds exceeding 270 miles (~430 kilometers) per hour? See *Bodies Exhibition*.
2 You can reach *Humor That Works* at 646-54-DREW-8.
3 Or you can join ACRONIM: the Acronym Cessation and Resistance Organization for Non–Idiomatic Messages

396. Connect Lists

When creating a list or agenda, try to tie each bullet point to a theme, such as song lyrics or movie titles.

397. Bet On It

Place friendly (non–monetary) bets on things like when projects will be completed or how much they'll cost. Bets could decide who creates your team's next presentation or takes meeting notes.

398. Present Blindly

Get a coworker's presentation and, without looking at it beforehand, try to present the material. Send your peer one of your presentations and see how they do.[1]

399. Ring Your Bell

Ring a bell every time you or someone in your department successfully completes a task.[2]

---

1 If you're really into it, Google "Battledecks" to find presentation competitions.
2 I learned this from a talk from Marcus Buckingham who shared how Best Buy did this with whistles: htww.co/whistle.

400. Get Buzzed

Play the corporate buzzword bingo drinking game!

Each time you hear one of the following words or phrases, you have to take a drink of water (or juice, or smoothie, or something that's healthy and not alcohol)[1]:

Alignment
Ballpark figure
Buzzword
Core competency
Exit strategy
Face time
Herding cats
Leverage
Long Tail
Outside the box

On the same page
Paradigm shift
Right sizing
Scale
Singe point-of-contact
Streamline
Synergy
Take it offline
Touch Base
Win-win

---

1 Find more at htww.co/buzzwords.

SKILL #5:
STRATEGIC DISENGAGEMENT

All work and no play makes Jack a dull boy. It also makes him likely to have problems in his personal life, likely to be quite boring, likely to be less effective than his coworkers, and very well likely to maybe die of stress–related illnesses. Humor not only helps Jack's dullness, but also keeps him healthy, wealthy, and wise.

Strategic Disengagement is just corporate terminology for taking a break, relaxing, and recharging the batteries. It helps to prevent burnout, improves concentration, and leads to more productivity in the long– (and often short–) run.

Most people strategically disengage at some level already (those two weeks of vacation, or two days over the weekend), but the work day doesn't have to be over to see the effects. Quick five–minute breaks (see #311) can go a long way in improving your effectiveness all day long.

Strategic Disengagement and Athletes

The term "Strategic Disengagement" comes from the Human Performance Institute[1], which studied world class athletes as a way to better understand how to make world class workers (referred to as "Corporate Athletes").

What they found, which will be no surprise to athletes, is that you reach peak performance not by exhausting yourself 100% of the time, or by sitting around doing nothing, but in oscillating between energy expenditure (such as working out) and energy renewal (resting).[2]

Which leads to an important point—not all stress is bad. Yes, chronic *distress* causes muscle tension, increases blood pressure, lowers immunity, and can cause anxiety, depression, sadness, and burnout.[3]

But there's also a good kind of stress, called *eustress*. It helps you develop skills and is the key becoming more efficient and more effective.

And regardless of what kind of stress you face, you need rest. Taking a break with humor helps you recharge the batteries, meaning you come back stronger, more focused, and re-energized for your work.

---

1 Learn more at htww.co/hpi.
2 After all, your muscles don't grow while you're working out, they grow while you're resting *after* you've worked out and are consuming chocolate milk (one of the best post-workout drinks).
3 See *Stressed in America*.

Humor and Strategic Disengagement

Using humor is a perfect way to mentally and physically take a break from your work. Short spurts of it throughout the day help you maintain energy levels and keep you productive, all while increasing your overall workplace satisfaction.

For the purposes of this book, we're going to think about strategic disengagement in terms of the benefits it provides, as defined below:

- **Energizer** – Increase your energy to complete a task.
- **Stress Reliever** – Combat the negative effects of stress during and/or after particularly stressful situations.
- **Physical Activity** – Improve long–term physical health and get blood and oxygen flowing through the body.
- **Mental Exercise** – Improve long–term mental health and work the brain to improve creativity and help prevent mental diseases.
- **Play** – Have fun, enjoy life.

With these benefits in mind, here are 100 ways to use humor to strategically disengage.

ENERGIZER

"It just keeps going and going and going..."
- The Energizer Bunny

Workdays can be long and grueling. Eight to twelve hour days are the norm for a lot of industries. In order to stay productive throughout the day and prevent burnout, sometimes you need a jolt of energy to be able to focus. Energizers can provide that energy boost (without the need for a 5-hour Energy drink).

Energizers that use humor not only reinvigorate you, they also add a little fun.

401. Celebrate a "Holiday"

Look up an arbitrary "Holiday" and celebrate it[1]. Create invitations, bake a cake, or decorate—all based on the holiday theme.

January 4: Trivia Day
January 16: Nothing Day
February 17: Acts of Kindness Day
February 28: Public Sleeping Day
March 14: National Pi Day
March 26: Make Up a Holiday Day
April 1: Fun at Work Day
April 14: Moment of Laughter Day
May 1: Mother Goose Day
May 4: Star Wars Day
June 3: Repeat Day Repeat Day
June 29: Hug Holiday

July 1: International Joke Day
July 28: Milk Chocolate Day
August 13: Left Handers' Day
August 27: Just Because Day
September 5: Be Late Day
September 21: Gratitude Day
October 7: World Smile Day
October 13: Skeptics Day?
November 17: World Peace Day
November 30: World Hello Day
December 7: Letter Writing Day
December 23: Festivus

---

1 Find more holidays at htww.co/holidays.

402. Attack a Snack

Eat a snack to boost your energy, such as: almonds, dried fruit, or peanut M&Ms. If possible, have a little fun with how you eat it.[1]

403. Have a Spot of Tea

Take an afternoon tea (or coffee) break. Drink out of the fancy cups you used in #187. Experiment with different flavors until you find your "cup of tea."

404. Read this Book

Lost at how to energize? Keep this and other humor books at your desk. Leaf through them when you need a break.

405. Break with Humor

Have a slideshow of funny pictures or quotations rotate on display during the breaks of your meeting or off–site.[2]

---

1 I like to toss peanuts in the air and catch them in my mouth. Just don't choke and don't forget to clean up the ones you miss.
2 For some great quotations, check out the book *50 Quotations on Humor* (I heard it was written by an awesome gentleman) or visit humorsoffice.com.

406. View a Photo

Look at inspiring photography on sites like Flickr or Boston.com, or review your own photographs for inspiration.

407. Reason with Yourself

Create a list of reasons why you work. Include serious and not-so-serious answers, such as "So I can buy the King-Sized candy bars instead of the bite size."[1]

408. Get Suggestions

Create a "humor suggestion box" and encourage employees to submit their own ideas of how to bring humor to work.

409. Search and Enjoy

Search Google (or visit www.humorthatworks.com) for energizer activities. Some of my favorites include: Zombie Tag, Bunny Bunny, Walk / Stop and Crazy 8s.[2]

---

1 This is a large part of why I work. That and other desserts. Oh, also family and stuff.
2 For an explanation of these energizers, visit htww.co/energizers.

410. Go to the Bag

Have everyone in your group brainstorm a random activity and write it down on a scrap of paper. Put them all in a bag. Whenever the energy in your group is low, pull a slip of paper out of the bag and do the activity.[1]

Here are some activities to get you started:

- Do 10 jumping jacks.
- Take 5 minutes to sit in silence.
- Lip sync to a song.
- Find a stranger. Introduce yourself.
- Perform a field sobriety Test.
- Make 5 distinct faces.
- Rhyme 10 different words aloud.

---

1 I learned this from my awesome peers at *ComedySportz*. Check out comedysportz.com to find fast, clean, competitive improv near you.

411. Make a Splash

Go to the bathroom sink and splash water on your face. Pretend like you're in a movie and just escaped some bad guys.

412. Recharge Like Superman

Take a break during the day and try to get 10–15 minutes out in the sun (don't forget your sunscreen).[1]

413. Crack Your Knuckles

Burst the bubbles in the synovial fluids surrounding your joints, aka, crack your knuckles. Just don't be too zealous about it.[2]

414. Burst Through

Do a short burst of physical movement: a quick set of jumping jacks, a few shadow–boxing jabs, shaking out your limbs, etc.

---

1 Too much sun is bad for you but getting some each day increases your Vitamin D and helps show other people you are not a vampire.
2 It won't cause arthritis, but extreme cracking may cause soft–tissue damage.

415. Walk a New Walk

Walk around the office with a different gait. Try bow–legged, sauntering, or "too cool for school" strides and see how your energy changes.

416. Bust a Move

Dance like no one is watching—in your car, in a stairwell, or in the elevator.[1]

417. Bust a Move Together

Or dance with your peers. Take turns picking a "song of the day," and, whenever you or someone on your team needs a break, turn on the song and sing/dance together.[2]

418. Drum Along

Get two pencils and work on your drumming skills (just be careful not to annoy your neighbors).

---

1 There's a number of benefits to this: burning calories, adding energy, having fun and, of course, entertaining the security guard watching the closed–circuit TV.
2 Hat tip to Monica G. for the suggestion.

419. Battle Rap

Have a rap battle with your coworkers.[1]

As an example, here's a ridiculous rap I just made up:

OK, OK, Listen. Here we go...

I jump on a mic like I jump to conclusions.
I see strange looks so let me clear the confusion.
My rhymes add up, like I'm using Excel.
And if there's any doubt, yo I'm 'bout to dispel.
Cuz I climb the corporate ladder with the greatest of ease,
And if you wanna know how, well it's none of your beez.
I leverage my words and scale I my discussion,
I'll hit a drum twice but won't suffer re–percussions.
It's coming to an end, like it's corn on the COB,
It's the close of business, but I should stick to my day job.

Drupac out.

---

1 Fun Fact: In some Inuit cultures, debates were solved via "song duels" where the two debating parties sang songs mocking the other person. The person with the best jabs won over the audience and won the argument. tl;dr: Some Inuit cultures settled arguments using rap battles. See *Inuit Culture*.

STRESS RELIEVER

"I try to take one day at time, but sometimes several days attack me at once."
- Jennifer Yane

Stress is a growing problem in the workplace: 80% of Americans feel stressed, with 39% saying that work is the biggest contributor[1]. And given the negative effects of too much stress, it's important to find ways to relieve stress during the workday.

Humor is anti-stress. It reverses all the negative effects we learned about in the chapter intro. Humor relaxes muscles, increases bloodflow, improves our immune system, and makes us happier. So why not choose humor for your health?[2]

---

1 See *Americans Stressed.*
2 See *Humor Benefits: Anti-Stress.*

420. Tweet Something

Express yourself in 140 characters or less through microblogging.

Here are some example tweets related to working:[1]

- *I remember being disappointed my first day at work when I learned 1on1s had nothing to do with basketball.*
- *If you want to get a job catching lobsters, you have to be good at net working.*
- *I sometimes wonder if I was destined to be a telephone repairman but I missed my calling.*
- *When I was a kid, I went to the doctor for a cut on my arm. He was so funny he left me in stitches.*
- *I made my workspace a puzzle. I call it a Rubik's Cubicle.*
- *A rookie cop who also raps: "give me a beat."*

---

1 From the book #drewtarvintweets available at htww.co/tweets.

421. Read Dramatically

Hold "dramatic readings" in the office. Have volunteers dramatically read things like corporate emails & memos, the newspaper, or children's books.

422. Eat and Be Merry

Have a "laugh lunch" and watch clips from a TV show like *The Office* or *Whose Line Is It Anyway.*[1]

423. Go Site-Seeing

Visit a humor site like humorsoffice.com or cracked.com.

424. Find and Collect

Create a laughter file—a collection of anything that makes you laugh. If it's physical, keep it at your desk. If it's online, bookmark it in your browser or using a service like *Delicious*. Return to it whenever you need a good laugh or to share with others.

---

1 If you haven't seen Colin Mochrie's "Arctic Tern" clip, go to htww.co/arctic right now.

425. Flip a Calendar

Get a humorous daily calendar. Take a moment to look at the entry each day.

426. Toon-In

If you have a stack of paper you have to go through, randomly throw in a printout of jokes or cartoons throughout the stack. When you get to the printout, take a quick break for a laugh.

427. Laugh Off-Site

Hire a comedian to perform at your next off-site.[1]

428. Bookend with Comedy

Listen to stand-up comedy on the way to or from the office. Some comedians to check out (caution—not all are SFW): *Louis C.K., Eddie Izzard, George Carlin, Brian Regan, Jim Gaffigan, Jerry Seinfeld, Ricky Gervais, Steve Martin, Bill Cosby.*

---

1 Need a comedian that knows how to handle a corporate audience? I know this hilarious guy. He's charming, too. Go to htww.co/joker.

429. Step Back and Stand-Up

When stressed out about something, take a step back and try to find the humor in the situation (even if just temporarily). Write down what your favorite comedian might say about it.

Here are some examples from some professionals[1]:

Brendon Walsh on Badges:
The last job I had, I had to wear this badge around my neck all day—like, a laminated badge. It's like a backstage pass to the crappiest concert ever invented.

Dan Naturman on Job Interviews:
Here's an example of something you never say at a job interview: "Can I have my resume back? It's my only copy."

Michael Somerville on College vs Corporate:
Can you imagine behaving the same way at your job as you did in college? Be on the phone at midnight like, "Dude, I got a $40 million business pitch due tomorrow. I haven't even started it."

1 Find a whole collection of jokes at jokes.com.

430. Look Like a Kid

Whenever you get stressed about your job, think about how a kid might view what you do. What would they get excited about? How would they do the work?

Thoughts kids might have about the workplace:

- You get to play on a computer all day.
- You have a chair with wheels you can spin around in.
- You get to pack or buy your own lunch.
- You can wear a cool headset like you're a pilot.
- You get to talk to people from all over the world.
- You have a badge like you work at a secret agency.
- The vending machine has S'mores Pop Tarts in it[1].

---

1 You don't have to be a kid to get excited about this one.

431. Think About the Worst

If things seem rotten, create a facetious list of things that could be worse. Have to do data entry? Could be worse—at least you're not using punch cards. Got a long week ahead? Could be worse—at least no one's said "looks like you've got a case of the Mondays."[1]

432. Slam Some Poetry

Vent how you're feeling through poetry or song lyrics.[2]

433. Sing Out Loud

Use your car ride home to sing aloud and decompress from the workday. Try some Tom Petty, Adele, or System of a Down.[3]

434. Ad Lib Your Music

Jam to one of your favorite songs at your desk while wearing headphones. Mentally ad–lib words to the song based on who and what you see.[4]

---

1 Sad there aren't any more examples left? Could be worse—at least there were two!
2 If you become a famous poet or singer, I expect to be a part of your posse.
3 "Yeah, I'm freeeeeeeeeeeeeeeeeeeeeeeeeeeeeeeeeeeeeeeeeeeeeeeeeeee, free fallin."
4 "Yeah, I'm reeeeeeeeeeeeeeeeeeeeeeeeeeeeeeeeeeeeeeeeeeeeeeeeeeee, re-installin."

435. Eavesdrop

Keep a list of humorous (whether intentionally or unintentionally) things customers, managers, or direct reports say. Submit them to OverheardintheOffice.com.

This is one of my favorite examples from the site:

10 AM Situational Ethics:

Coworker #1: Can you believe the whole company needs to take an ethics exam? It's online, but still...

Coworker #2: Yeah, it sucks. I heard one department's doing the whole thing on a conference call together.

Coworker #1: But there's a test...

Coworker #2: Yeah, they're all taking the test together. One person says the answer and everybody enters it on their screen after the first person confirms it's right.

436. Smell the Roses

Take a break to take in your surroundings using all five senses. What can you see from your desk? What can you hear? What can you smell? What can you feel? What can you taste?[1]

437. Open a "Window"

Look longingly out a window. If you're in an office with few views of the outdoors, setup a webcam outside and livestream it to an internal website for people to use as their "window."[2]

438. Grow Life

Get a plant. Water it. Care for it. Talk to it.[3]

439. Make It a Dog Day

Take a break to play with a pet; if you don't have one, stop by a friend's house or a dog park.

---

1 If you have the Sixth Sense, maybe avoid telling people and freaking them out.
2 This was done by some of my geeky friends at P&G. I wish I still had that view.
3 There is some truth to talking to plants to help them grow. Scientists speculate it's either because of the carbon dioxide, or plants responding to the vibration of sound.

440. Breathe

Take 10 deep breaths every hour.

A number of studies suggest just taking deep breaths can lead to a smorgasboard of health benefits.

Deep breathing:

- May reduce anxiety.[1]
- Has been shown to relieve trauma symptoms.[2]
- Can reduce blood pressure.[3]
- Can alleviate back pain.[4]
- Reduces short–term pain and may help with chronic pain.[5]

Need help focusing? Visit www.take10deepbreaths.com.

---

1 See *Performance Anxiety.*
2 See *A Breath of Relief.*
3 See *Breathe Deep.*
4 See *Deep Breathing for Back Pain.*
5 See *Breathing Deeply.*

PHYSICAL ACTIVITY

"I like to move it, move it."
- Reel 2 Real

The majority of corporate employees spend 5–6 hours sitting every workday. This sedentary lifestyle can cause physical health issues if not combated. Frequent breaks throughout the day can keep your body physically healthy, making you more productive in the short and long-term.

Humor can make that physical activity more enjoyable, increasing the likelihood you'll actually do it.

441. Live and Laugh

Try to laugh 100 times in a day; it doesn't matter at what.

Laughing 10–15 minutes per day can help you lose up to four pounds (1.8 kg) per year[1], and burns as many calories as[2]:

- 5 Minutes of Jogging
- 5 minutes of High Impact Aerobics
- 5 minutes of Boxing / Sparring
- 10 Minutes of Yoga
- 10 Minutes of Dancing
- 15 Minutes of Walking
- 15 Minutes of Cleaning
- 15 Minutes of Milking a Cow
- 20 Minutes of Ice Fishing
- 20 Minutes of Playing the Cello

---

1 See *Energy Expenditure of Genuine Laughter.*
2 See *Laugh Yourself Skinny* and *Calories Burned During Exercise.*

442. Sit Weird

Try sitting on the front of your seat or on an exercise ball to force good posture. Or "sit" really weird and use a standing desk.[1]

443. Get Up and Down

Stand up. Sit down.[2]

444. Walk Around

Start a walking group at work; map out a route through the office that has you walking for at least 10 minutes.

445. Race a Coworker

When the office is empty, race a coworker in your chairs.

---

1 Some studies suggest that sitting 6+ hours a day means you are 40% more likely to die within 15 years than someone who sits less than 3 hours a day. When sitting, electrical activity in your legs shuts off, you only burn 1 calorie per minute and your good cholesterol drops by 20%. See *Sitting All Day is Killing You*.
2 Congratulations, you've just burned 2 calories and increased your heart rate!

446. Play Toss

Find a partner and go into a hallway and toss a football or bouncy ball back and forth. Use an imaginary one if you can't find or use a real one.

447. Touch Once

While on break at an offsite, play One–Touch with people: see how long you can keep a ball (or even a crumpled piece of paper) in the air by hitting it. The only rule is that the same person can't hit it twice in a row.

448. Workout

Use your lunchbreak to workout at your local gym.

449. Fill a Knead

Get a massage at the end of the day. Even better, have your group hire a masseuse to come in during the day and allow people to take breaks for a massage.[1]

1 *Google*, *Boeing*, and others have done this and tout incredible benefits, not just for employees but also the bottom line. One study showed office workers who received regular massages were more alert, less stressed, and performed better. See *Massage*.

450. Release Pressure

If you don't have time to go to a masseuse, or can't convince your company to bring one in, do it yourself!

Here are some good points to massage[1]:

- Stroke your left shoulder area with your right hand, going from the skull down to the elbow. Switch sides.
- Use circular motions to massage either side of your spine. Move up to the back of the skull behind the ears.
- Use circular motions on each of your fingers. Massage between your thumb and pointer finger.
- Lightly massage the temple near your eyebrows.
- With a closed fist, lightly "punch" your quads, hamstrings and calves.

---

1 Find more exercises at htww.co/selfmassage.

451. Stretch Yourself

Do stretches at your desk. They can be anything, like the classic "arm–over–back–of–the–head" or "neck–from–side–to–side."[1]

452. Nibble

Stretch the face muscle by eating something every two hours. "Nibblers" statistically weigh less than "Gorgers."[2]

453. Eat a Fistful

Your stomach is the same size as one to two of your fists. As a result, a general rule for controlling how much you eat is that no portion of any one thing should be larger than one fist.

454. Taste the Rainbow

Throughout the day, try to eat fruits and vegetables from each of the colors in the rainbow.

---

1 You can also visit htww.co/stretching for more official stretches with pictures.
2 Eating smaller meals more often (as opposed to 2–3 larger meals) helps maintain your metabolism and keeps your glycemic index from spiking too high or dropping too low. See *Nibblers and Gorgers*.

455. Get Gummy

Buy Gummy vitamins. Eat two every day after lunch.[1]

456. Break to Hydrate

Always have water at your desk. When your cup is empty, use it as an excuse to leave your desk to get some more.

457. Go on Mute

When your voice is strained, challenge yourself to go the entire day without speaking.

458. Lookout for Your Eyes

Take care of your eyes and reduce eyestrain by following the 20/20/20 rule: Every 20 minutes look at something 20 feet away for at least 20 seconds.[2]

---

1 I guess you could take regular vitamins. But if there's a gummy version, why wouldn't you choose it?

2 If one minute every hour is too much time for good eye health, at least try to blink more often or change your monitor display settings for better eye care. I'd hate for you to be unable to read this book!

459. Sleep

Take a nap at work.

No, seriously. In a Harvard Business Review article titled *Why Companies Should Insist that Employees Take Naps*, author Tony Schwartz shares[1]:

- Naps improve perceptual skills, motor skills, reaction time, and alertness.
- Naps can help sustain performance all day long, rather than having a typical drop-off in the afternoon.
- Naps improve memory retention.

To properly nap in the workplace:

- The nap should be 30 minutes or less.
- The best time for it is between 1pm and 3pm.
- Don't stress about "falling asleep." Just close your eyes and slow your breathing.

---

1 See *Insist Employees Take Naps*.

MENTAL EXERCISE

Calvin: "I've been thinking, Hobbes."
Hobbes: "On a weekend?"
Calvin: "Well it wasn't on purpose."
- Calvin and Hobbes

In addition to improving creativity now, mental exercise is key to keeping the brain healthy for the later years of life. Studies show that simple mental exercises help ward off brain diseases such as Alzheimer's and dementia[1].

Humor exercises the brain by challenging it in a fun and playful way.

---

1 See *Using the Brain*.

460. Sign Up for Knowledge

Sign up for a humorous newsletter such as *Now I Know* or *delanceyplace* and use their emails as an excuse to take a break and learn something new.[1]

461. Listen to TED

Learn something awesome from a video on TED (www.ted.com) or Big Think (www.bigthink.com).

462. Say the Word

Check out Merriam–Webster's word of the day; see if you can naturally work it into a conversation.[2]

463. Know What's Going On

Schedule 30 minutes on your calendar every week to read about what's happening in your industry.

---

1 Joel Schwartz, retired psychiatrist, speaker, and author of www.stresslessshrink.com, suggests the *Humor That Works* Newsletter (he said it, not me). To sign up for these great newsletters and more, check out: htww.co/newsletters.
2 I hope this book makes you happy enough to *rollick* around and results in *ataraxia*.

464. Learn Today

Browse "Today I Learned" on *reddit* for a new nugget of wisdom. Just go to reddit.com/r/TodayILearned.

Some interesting things I've learned:

- The average NFL game features just 10 minutes and 43 seconds of action. The rest is commercials, replays, and shots of the players huddling.
- The original surveyors of Mount Everest lied and added 2 feet to its height to make it 29,002 feet, because they didn't think people would believe them if they said it was really 29,000 feet high.
- Bill Murray doesn't have an agent, just an 800 number that you call and leave a voicemail pitching your movie.
- Prior to WWII in the United States, Einstein was so well-known that people regularly stopped him on the street to inquire about his theories, to which he began replying, "Pardon me, I am often mistaken for Professor Einstein."

465. Think Outside the Cube

Learn to solve a Rubik's cube.[1] Solve it periodically while on conference calls, encourage people to come by your desk and mess it up, or teach others how to solve it.

You can also explain how a Rubik's cube is a great metaphor for life:

- It's no fun if you just sit there not doing anything.
- Sometimes when you get one part of your life straightened out, it messes up another part.
- It takes planning, patience, and a little bit of luck to figure everything out.
- Inevitably, once you do have it all figured out, someone comes along and messes it all up.

---

1 To do it, there are a series of algorithms to follow and once you learn them, you can solve a cube no matter how "messed up" it is: htww.co/rubiks.

466. Master the Paper Arts

Learn to make an origami crane, then make one while you are on a conference call or give them to new members of your team.[1]

467. Stare at Something

Get a *Magic Eye* book for your cubicle. Find your favorite images and share them with people when they come by.[2]

468. Take Notice

Improve your observation skills and try to notice something new in your office every few days, e.g. details of the ceiling pattern, the type of carpet, or what's hanging in different people's cubicles.

469. Re-route Your Travel

Explore a different way to or from work.

---

1 You can find out how to make a crane here: htww.co/crane.
2 The official name of these images is "stereogram." To find out more (or learn how to create your own) check out: htww.co/stereogram.

470. Be Non-Dominant

Take a little more time on your lunch break and eat using your non-dominant hand during lunch.[1]

471. Crunch Numbers

Solve a Sudoku puzzle in between meetings or work out some simple math problems: 2+85 = ? 6x13 = ? ((8+2-15)*18)/-9 = ?[2]

472. Get Carded

Play a mind game with a coworker, like *Old Maid* or *Set*.

473. Get TypeCast

Return to your elementary school ways and get better at typing by playing a game.[3] Or you can just force yourself to touch-type by covering your hands and not looking at the keyboard.

---

1 This forces the brain to work harder, creating new neurons and forcing it to think differently, both of which can increase creativity and may help stave off Alzheimer's.
2 Answers: eighty-seven; seventy-eight; ten.
3 My favorite typing games: htww.co/typing.

474. Quiz Yourself

Take a couple of fun quizzes or answer trivia questions at a site like Sporcle (www.sporcle.com).

Here are two of my favorite trivia questions:

- In the United States, there are four states whose capital starts with the same letter as the state name. Name them.[1]
- Between the NHL, NBA, NFL, and MLB, there are 9 sports teams whose name does *not* end with "s." Name them.[2]

---

1 Dover, DE; Indianapolis, IN; Oklahoma City, OK; Honolulu, HI.
2 NHL: *Colorado Avalanche, Minnesota Wild, Tampa Bay Lightning;*
NBA: *Miami Heat, Oklahoma City Thunder, Orlando Magic, Utah Jazz;*
NFL: *None;*
MLB: *Boston Red Sox, Chicago White Sox.*

475. Associate Freely

Do free word association based on objects you can see in the office.

This exercise is often done when teaching improv as a way to demonstrate how different people have different initial reactions. For example, for each of the words listed below, say aloud the first word that comes to mind. Compare that to my list in the footnotes[1].

(1) Tree	(6) Exit
(2) Fire	(7) Shatter
(3) Grip	(8) Orange
(4) Tornado	(9) List
(5) License	(10) Andrew

---

1 (1) House; (2) Aim; (3) Strength; (4) Spin; (5) to Kill; (6) Fast; (7) Destroy; (8) Yes; (9) Make; (10) ME!.

476. Say Dada

Create a Dada monologue. Try to say a monologue of words that don't make any sense and don't relate to each other.[1]

477. Memorize Something

Work on your memory skills by memorizing something: a monologue from a play, the lyrics to a song, my website URL, email, and phone number…[2]

478. Be Instrumental

Play an instrument. If it's allowed, play it in a breakroom at work. If not, play in your car, at home, or use a virtual instrument like in *Garage Band,* or an online drum kit.

479. Think About Nothing

Meditate.[3]

---

1 This is surprisingly difficult because our mind works using associations. Avoid listing things and any time you notice you're saying words from one category, switch it up.
2 www.humorthatworks.com | andrew@humorthatworks.com | 646-543-7398
3 Studies show a number of benefits to meditating. Find out more at htww.co/meditate.

480. Smile

That's it, just Smile.[1]

---

1 A smile can reduce stress and help you feel better. See *Simply Smiling*.

PLAY

"There is work that is work and there is play that is play; there is play that is work and work that is play. And in only one of these lies happiness."
- Gelett Burgess

There are only 168 hours in a week. If you spend a minimum of 40 hours a week at work, that's 25% of your adult life spent in the corporate office. Do you really want to relegate play to only the weekends? Simply taking a break and doing something for fun can go a long way in improving your productivity and happiness.

Humor is play; it keeps us young and having fun.

481. Sport Up the Office

Invent an office sport. Play it with your coworkers.

The following is a list of office sports I've played:

- **Trash Cube** — Shoot ice cubes into the garbage can.
- **Stress Ball Bowling** — Use a stress ball to knock down "pins" made from various office supplies.
- **Chair Spinning** — Attempt to get the most number of rotations spinning in a chair.
- **Thumb Tack Plinko** — Create a Plinko board on your cubicle wall with thumb tacks. Drop a penny down it.
- **Garbage Horse** — Play the basketball game *Horse* by shooting old paper into a recycling bin.

482. Play Mini Golf

Set up a mini golf course in the office. Use office supplies and other materials to create obstacles (bonus points for a windmill).[1]

483. Take Aim

Use the dartboard from #244 and have a darts tournament. I enjoy *Cricket*, *Golf* and, in honor of this book, *501*.

484. Score a Touchdown

Play paper football while waiting for a meeting to start.[2]

485. Share Some XOXOs

Play tic–tac–toe with a coworker. Hint: If you go first ("X"), always play a corner. If you go second ("O") play the center (if that's taken, play a corner).

---

1 I heard about this from Matt Weinstein's newsletter (subscribe at htww.co/weinstein). One team at *Electronic Data Systems* created an entire 18–hole course. They charged other departments a "greens fee" to play and used the money to sponsor a Happy Hour.
2 To learn how to make a paper football, check out: htww.co/paperfootball.

486. Hit the Deck

Order a personalized deck of cards for your work; play *Go Fish*, *Speed*, or *Solitaire* with them.

487. Tell the Future

Build a "Paper Fortune Teller." Write down work–related fortunes such as "You will get a raise," "New projects are in your future," or "Someone will change your desktop picture to *My Little Ponies*."[1]

488. Build Office Supply Art

Grab some office supplies and build something with them, ideally in a way that you could take it apart and use the supplies if you needed to. My personal favorite is the pen bow and arrow.[2]

489. Build with Legos

Keep Legos in the breakroom. Allow people to build anything they want with them.

---

1 To learn how to build a Paper Fortune Teller: htww.co/fortuneteller.
2 For inspiration, check out htww.co/officesupplyart.

490. Board Games

In addition to the Legos, leave various board games like *Battleship* in the breakroom and challenge people to play.[1]

One of my favorite board games is *Tri-Bond*, where you are given three clues that all relate to one answer.

As an example, *Popcorn*, *Military* and *Corn* all have kernels (colonels).

Can you guess these office-related ones[2]:

1. Swingline fillable; Office supply store; Routine food.
2. Computer; Mighty; *Matrix* character.
3. Suite; Branch; Chief.
4. Pictures; Stars; Strategies.
5. Bad mic sound; Critiques; Chickens returning food.

---

1 I don't recommend playing *Monopoly*. You'll either never finish the game or your work, and you'll make some enemies in the process.
2 Answers: (1) Staples; (2) Mouse; (3) Executive; (4) Align; (5) Feedback.

491. Guess Who

Play *Guess Who* in a meeting[1].

The instructions are easy:

1. Get two volunteers to help you. Have them come to the front of the room.
2. Tell everyone else to stand up.
3. Pick someone from the crowd, but don't say who it is.
4. Volunteer #1 asks a "Yes or No" question to narrow down the possibilities ("Is this person a boy?"). If you say yes, all the people that match the criteria remain standing; if you say no, all the people who match the criteria sit down.
5. Volunteer #2 then asks a "Yes or No" question and again you answer based on who you picked and the corresponding group stays standing or sits down.
6. Alternate between #4 and #5 until only a handful of people are remaining and one of the volunteers correctly guesses who you picked in #3.

---

1 If you want to practice, order the game *Guess Who*: htww.co/guesswho.

492. Voiceover a Conversation

Take a break and play *Voiceover* with 2 people you see having a conversation—ignore what they are actually saying and add in your own dialogue of what they could be talking about.[1]

493. Caption Photos

Post photos in a common area; encourage people to write funny captions or speech bubbles on them.

494. Take a Photo

Better yet, take a break and try to take some artistic photos in your office or outside.[2]

495. Chalk It Up

Paint a wall with chalkboard paint. Allow employees to share expressions of gratitude, write humorous (but appropriate) sayings, or just have some fun and draw.

---

1 For added fun, do this with a peer. Create characters for each person (be nice).
2 You can also offer to take "headshots" for your coworkers (think *Glamour Shots*).

496. Vandalize

Add humorous adjustments to signs in your office space (just make sure they aren't permanent).

Some examples I've seen[1]:

- On a stairwell marked "Stairway 2" someone added "Heaven" underneath it.
- On a "Door Out of Order" sign, someone added "Temporarily a Wall."
- On a door labeled "Mechanical Shaft," someone added "Who's the robot that won't cop out when there's danger all about?"
- On a "Beware of Dog" sign, someone added "He is very sarcastic."
- On a Pedestrian Detour sign, one person added "Walk This Way" and another person added "Talk this Way."

---

1 For even more, check out htww.co/funnysigns.

497. Give a Makeover

Give a work friend an online makeover using Photoshop or an online tool like Taaz (www.taaz.com).[1]

498. Loosen Your Feet

Dance, just with your feet, while sitting down at your desk. Try tap dancing, Riverdancing, or c-walking (they're all much easier when sitting down).

499. Secretly Agent

Pretend like you're a spy when you're walking through the halls. Duck below cubicle walls, hug the corners, and peek around corners. Hum the *Mission Impossible* theme.

500. Vilify Yourself

Lean back in your chair and put your hands together (or stroke an invisible cat) like a James Bond villain.[2]

---

1 Yes, even if the person is a man.
2 Chuckling to yourself is optional. Maniacal laughter may cause some suspicion.

THE FINAL WAY

Thus far, we've covered 500 ways you can use humor to improve communication, build relationships, enhance problem solving, increase productivity, and strategically disengage.

That's a lot of ways—if you used one way every single workday of the year, assuming five-day work weeks and two weeks of vacation, you'd go two years before repeating one.

But that's not the end. Not for someone as smart, humorous, and as attractive as you. This list of 500 is just inspiration—a way to get you thinking about finding your own way to add humor to the workplace.

With regard to humor at work, *what* you do isn't nearly as important as *that* you do... something, anything, everything (just not all at once).

501. Humor Yourself

Brainstorm your own way to use humor in the workplace.[1]

It's not as hard as it seems—just think about what you find fun and find a way to incorporate it into your work.

Assuming you follow the general guidelines in the first chapter, you'll have no problem coming up with humor that is not only fun, but also effective at work.

You've learned to have fun your whole life: as a kid, teenager, college student, and even as an adult. You've discovered things you enjoy doing, things that make you laugh and smile.

Take those things, and that personality, with you when you go to work in the morning and humor yourself.

You deserve it / want it/ need it.

---

1 Got a great idea you want to share? Submit it at htww.co/submit so others can learn about your humor genius!

ABOUT THE AUTHOR

Andrew Tarvin

Andrew Tarvin is an award–winning speaker, author, and coach. Through *Humor That Works*, he teaches individuals and organizations how to effectively use humor in the workplace.

He is the author of 4 books, including this one you've just finished reading (or skipped to the end of). He has written more than 400 posts on business topics such as humor, productivity, and strategic disengagement, garnering more than 1.5 million pageviews from 180 countries.

Andrew lives in New York City, loves the color orange, and is obsessed with milkshakes.

To book Andrew for an engagement, contact consulting@humorthatworks.com or call 646-543-7398.

ABOUT HUMOR THAT WORKS

www.HumorThatWorks.com

Humor That Works is dedicated to teaching individuals and organizations how to use humor to be more effective, more productive, and more awesome.

We offer keynote speaking, hands–on training, and one–on–one coaching on a variety of topics including: humor in the workplace, improving communication, building relationships, enhancing creativity, increasing productivity, and strategically disengaging.

Humor That Works has worked with more than 50 different organizations ranging from large corporations like *Procter & Gamble* to small businesses like *Basco Manufacturing*.

For more, visit www.humorthatworks.com.

ACKNOWLEDGMENTS

To my family for all of their support over the years. To Mom for her sense of humor and for those times we spent making up puns based on what store we were going to. To Dad for his sense of humor and sarcasm. To Adam for his practical jokes and good–natured pranks. And to David for always teaching me, even when what he was teaching was completely made up.

To Pat for his help writing and editing. To Nate for getting me involved in this whole comedy thing and ~~ruining~~ changing my life. To Woodruff for always challenging me even when I didn't want him to.

To everyone in *The 8th Floor*, past and present; to the great folks at *ComedySportz* and *The Magnet*; and to my friends in NYC who remind me to take a break every once and awhile.

To the great people I've met through the *Humor Project, AATH*, and *AIN*, for their inspiration, guidance, and knowledge of humor.

To all the people at *P&G* who put up with all my trials and errors while attempting to use humor. To my managers, Jonathan, John, Andrea, Pablo, Hilmar, Jose, and Dave for encouraging the pursuit of my passion. To Josh and Rajiv for all of the mentorship and for showing me what's possible.

And of course, to you, the reader.

SOURCES

Below are the sources referenced throughout the book (in alphabetical order). You can also find these sources, along with links, at htww.co/sources.

A Breath of Relief. Gerbarg, Patricia L. and Richard P. Brown. "Yoga: A breath of relief for Hurricane Katrina refugees," *Current Psychiatry*, Vol 4, 2005. [pg 232]

Ambient awareness. "Ambient awareness," Wikipedia.org, Retrieved JUL 2012. [pg 106]

Ambient Noise and Creative Cognition. Mehta, Ravi and Rui Zhu. "Is Noise Always Bad? Exploring the Effects of Ambient Noise on Creative Cognition," *Journal of Consumer Research*, Vol 39, DEC 2012. [pg 131]

Americans Stressed. Traynor, Kate. "80% of Americans Feel Stressed," *American Society of Health-System Pharmacists*, 2003. [pg 223]

Blink. Gladwell, Malcolm. *Blink: The Power of Thinking Without Thinking.* Back Bay Books, 2007. [pg 142]

Bodies Exhibition. From *Bodies: The Exhibition Exhibit* in New York, Retreived SEP 2011. [pg 207]

Brain Rules. Medina, John. *Brain Rules: 12 Principles for Surviving and Thriving at Work, at Home, and School.* Pear Press, 2009. [pg 33]

Brave New World of Digital Intimacy. Thompson, Clive. "Brave New World of Digital Intimacy," *The New York Times*, SEP 2008. [pg 106]

Breathe Deep. "Breathe deep to lower blood pressure," *Associated Press*, JUL 2006. [pg 232]

Breathing Deeply. "How breathing deeply can reduce pain," *Mail Online, dailymail.co.uk*, Retrieved SEP 2012. [pg 232]

Calories Burned During Exercise. "Calories Burned During Exercise," *nutristrategy.com*, Retrieved SEP 2011. [pg 234]

Coping with Distractions. Cohen, Yaacov. "Coping with Distractions: 6 Ways You Can Boost Your Productivity," *Forbes.com,* Retrieved JUN 2012. [pg 181]

Creative pause. Moll, Cameron. "Why thinking in the shower may be an ideal model for 'creative pause'" *CameronMoll.com*, Retrieved OCT 2012. [pg 132]

Deep Breathing for Back Pain. Ng, Nick. "Deep-Breathing Exercises for Back Pain," *Livestrong.com,* Retrieved SEP 2012. [pg 232]

Definition of Amusement. "amusement," *Dictionary.com*, Retrieved FEB 21, 2010. [pg 2]

Definition of Communication. "communication," *Dictionary.com.* Retrieved FEB 21, 2010 [pg 13]

Definition of Humor. "humor," *Dictionary.com*, Retrieved FEB 21, 2010. [pg 2]

Definition of Relationships. "relationship," *Dictionary.com,* Retrieved FEB 21, 2010 [pg 61]

Diversity and Creativity. McLeod, Poppy L. and Sharon A. Lobel. "Ethnic Diversity and Creativity in Small Groups," *Small Group Research*, Vol 27, 1996 [pg 126]

Energy Expenditure of Genuine Laughter. Buchowski, Maciej. "Energy Expenditure of Genuine Laughter," *International Journal of Obesity,* 2005. [pg 234]

Feelings and Predictions. Katz, Joseph M. and Michel Tuan Pham. "Feeling the Future: The Emotional Oracle Effect," *Journal of Consumer Research*, OCT 2012. [pg 142]

Haiku in English. "Haiku in English," *Wikipedia.org*, Retrieved SEP 2012. [pg 53]

How Much Wood. "How much wood would a woodchuck chuck if a woodchuck could chuck wood?" *Answers, wiki.answers.com*, Retrieved OCT 2012. [pg 206]

Humor and Performance. Breeze, L. and A. Dawson."Humor in the Workplace: Anecdotal Evidence Suggests Connection to Employee Performance," *Perspectives in Business*, St Edwards University, 2004 [pg 163]

Humor Benefits: Anti-Stress. Toffelmire, Amy. "Ha! Laughing is Good for You!" *Canoe.ca*, Retrieved APR 2009. [pgs 6, 223]

Humor Benefits: Be Happy. Valliant, George E. *Aging Well*. Little, Brown & Company, 2002. [pg 7]

SOURCES

Humor Benefits: Be in Control. Craumer, Martha. "Getting Serious About Workplace Humor," *Harvard Communication Letter*, JUL 2002. [pg 7]

Humor Benefits: Builds Trust. Vartabedian, RA and Laurel Klinger Vartabedian. "Humor in the Workplace: A Communication Challenge," presented at the *Speech Communication Association*, Miami, Florida, NOV, 1993. [pg 7]

Humor Benefits: Burn Calories. Griffin, R. Morgan. "Give Your Body a Boost," *WebMD.com*, Retrieved AUG 27, 2011. [pg 6]

Humor Benefits: Do Better Job. Bannister, Steve. "Making Sense of Humour in the Workplace," *Enterprise Magazine*, NOV 2006. [pg 7]

Humor Benefits: Higher Intelligence. Hauck, William E. "The Relationship of Humor to Intelligence, Creativity, and Intentional and Incidental Learning," *The Journal of Experimental Education*, Summer 1972. [pg 6]

Humor Benefits: Improves Brainpower. McMaster, Robyn. "A Dash of Humor Ups Performance and Creativity at Work," *Brain Based Biz*, SEP 2008. [pg 6]

Humor Benefits: Improves Retention. Garner, Randy. "Humor, Analogy, and Metaphor: H.A.M. it up in Teaching," *Radical Pedagogy*, 2005. [pgs 6, 41]

Humor Benefits: Increase Efficiency. Abramis, David. "All Work and No Play Isn't Even Good for Work," *Psychology Today*, MAR 1989. [pg 6]

Humor Benefits: Increase Opportunities. Buhler, Patricia. "Wanted: Humor in the Workplace," *Supervision,* Vol 52, 1991. [pg 7]

Humor Benefits: Increases Creativity. Isen, Alice M. "Positive affect facilitates creative problem solving," *Journal of Personality and Social Psychology,* 1987. [pgs 6, 125]

Humor Benefits: Make More Money. Robert, Christopher. "The Case for Developing New Research on Humor and Culture in Organizations," *Research in Personnel and Human Resources Management*, Vol 26, 2007 [pg 7]

Humor Benefits: Prevent Heart Disease. Seiler, Bill. "Laughter Helps Blood Vessels," *University of Maryland Medical Center*, MAR 2005. [pg 6]

Humor in the Workplace. Cronin, R. "Humor in the Workplace." Study by *Hodge-Cronin and Associates*, 1997. [pg 4]

Iconoclast. Berns, Gregory. *Iconoclast: A Neuroscientist Reveals How to Think Differently*. Harvard Business Review Press, 2010. [pg 131]

Insist Employees Take Naps. Schwartz, Tony. "Why Companies Should Insist That Employees Take Naps," *HBR Blog Network*, SEP, 2010. [pg 240]

Introduction to Problem Solving. Harris, Robert. "Introduction to Problem Solving," *VirtualSalt*. JUL 1998. [pg 111]

Inuit Culture. "The Inuit Way: A Guide to Inuit Culture," Produced by *Pauktuutit Inuit Women of Canada*, 2006. [pg 222]

Laugh Yourself Skinny. "Go Ahead -- Laugh Yourself Skinny," *Daily News Central, dailynewscentral.com*, Retrieved SEP 2011. [pg 234]

Laughing All the Way to the Bank. Sala, Fabio. "Laughing All the Way to the Bank," *Harvard Business Review*, SEP 2003. [pg 113]

Laughing All the Way to the Bedroom. Greengross, Gil. "Laughing All the Way to the Bedroom," *Psychology Today*, May 1, 2011. [pg 5]

Let the Good Times Roll. Stauffer, David. "Let the Good Times Roll: Building a Fun Culture," *Harvard Management Update*, OCT 1998. [pg 62]

Massage. Field, Tiffany and Gail Ironson. "Massage therapy reduces anxiety and enhances EEG pattern of alertness and math computations." *International Journal of Neuroscience*, Vol 86, SEP 1996. [pg 236]

Master the Silent Language. Borg, James. *Body Language: 7 Easy Lessons to Master the Silent Language*. FT Press, 2010. [pg 22]

McLuhan. "Tetrad of media effects," *Wikipedia.org*, Retrieved SEP 2012. [pg 155]

Music and Productivity. Iwanaga, Makota. "Subjective and Physiological Responses to Music Stimuli," *Journal of Music Therapy*, XXXVI, 1996 [pg 197]

Neural responses to giving. Harbaugh, William T. and Ulrich Mayr. "Neural responses to taxation and voluntary giving reveal motives for charitable donations," *Science*, 316, 2007. [pg 80]

Nibblers and Gorgers. Southgate, D. A. "Nibblers, gorgers, snackers, and grazers," *British Medical Journal*, Volume 300, JAN 1990. [pg 238]

Office Ergonomics. "Office ergonomics: Your how-to guide," *The Mayo Clinic*, mayoclinic.com, Retrieved SEP 2012. [pg 193]

SOURCES

Optimal Philanthropy for Human Beings. Muehlhauser, Luke. "Optimal Philanthropy for Human Beings," *LessWrong.com*, Retreived JUL 2012. [pg 80]

Parkinson's Law. Parkinson, C. Northcote. "Parkinson's Law," *The Economist*, NOV 1955. [pg 162]

Performance Anxiety. Jacobs, Tom. "Performance Anxiety? Take a Deep Breath." *Pacific Standard Magazine*, OCT 2012. [pg 232]

Problem solving. "Problem solving," *Wikipedia.org*, Retrieved AUG 2012. [pg 111]

Proprietary Eponyms. "Generic trademark," *Wikipedia.org*, Retrieved OCT 2012. [pg 152]

Prosocial spending and well-being. Aknin, Lara B. and Christopher P. Barrington-Leigh. "Prosocial spending and well-being," *NBER Working Paper* 16415, 2010. [pg 80]

Pursuing sustained happiness. Lyubomirsky, Sonja and Chris. "Pursuing sustained happiness through random acts of kindness and counting one's blessings," *Department of Psychology*, University of California, 2004. [pg 80]

Secret of Employee Recognition. Bersin, Josh. "New Research Unlocks the Secret of Employee Recognition," *Forbes.com*, Retrieved SEP 2012. [pg 78]

Simply Smiling. Stromberg, Joseph. "Simply Smiling Can Actually Reduce Stress," *Smithsonian Magazine*, JUL 2012. [pg 250]

Sitting All Day is Killing You. Johnson, Dave. "Why sitting all day is killing you," *CBS News*, *cbsnews.com*, Retrieved SEP 2012. [pg 235]

Smile and Put Warmth into your Phone Calls. "Smile and Put Warmth Into Your Phone Calls," *HP Newsroom*, Retrieved JUN 2012. [pg 21]

Snap Decisions. McKendrick, Joe. "'Snap' decisions may be just as effective as well-informed decisions," *Smartplanet.com*, Retrieved SEP 2012. [pg 142]

Space Invaders. "Space Invaders," *Wikipedia.org*, Retrieved OCT 2012. [pg 140]

Statistics on New Year's Resolutions. Norcross, John C. and Marci S. Myrkalo. "Auld Lang Syne: Success predictors, change processes, and self-reported outcomes of New Year's resolvers and nonresolvers." *Journal of Clinical Psychology*, Vol 58, 2002. [pg 177]

Stressed in America. Clay, R.A. "Stressed in America," *American Psychological Association*, Vol 42, JAN 2011. [pg 212]

Teamwork and Job Satisfaction. Kalisch, Beatrice J. and Hyunhwa Lee. "Nursing staff teamwork and job satisfaction," *Journal of Nursing Management*, Vol 18, 2010. [pg 91]

The Effective Executive. Drucker, Peter F. *The Effective Executive.* HarperBusiness, 2006. [pg 187]

The Importance of Community. APS Healthcare. "The Importance of Community." *Washington. edu*, Retrieved JUN 2012. [pg 81]

The Man Behind the Vacuum Cleaner. Varrasi, John. "The Man Behind the Vacuum Cleaner," *ASME KnowledgeBase*, DEC 2011. [pg 127]

The Protégé Effect. Paul, Annie Murphy. "The Protégé Effect," *Time Ideas*, NOV 2011. [pg 186]

The Story Behind Service with a Smile. Johnson, Hazel-Anne. "The story behind service with a smile." *Graduate School Theses & Dissertations*, University of South Florida, JUN 2004. [pg 21]

Unique Origins. "The Unique Origins of 25 Popular Products," *BusinessPundit.com*, Retrieved SEP 2012. [pg 152]

Using the Brain. Haederle, Michael. "Exercising the Body, Using the Brain May Ward Off Alzheimer's Disease," *AARP Bulletin*, FEB 2012. [pg 241]

WMSD Prevention. "Work-Related Musculoskeletal Disorders (WMSDs) Prevention," *Centers for Disease Control and Prevention, cdc.gov*, Retrieved OCT 2012. [pg 193]

Write It Down. "Write It Down: Note-Taking Effectiveness and the Digital Classroom Revolution," *Course Hero*, Retrieved JUL 2012. [pgs 44, 50]

I would be remiss if I didn't also mention a few other "sources:"

- Various humorists/speakers/authors who have shared countless humor tips over the years, including: Joel Goodman, Mike Kerr, Kat Koppett, Patricia Ryan Madson, and many more.
- Groups and organizations who have taught me countless improv exercises, including: *ComedySportz*, the *Applied Improv Network*, *Smarty Pants*, and quite a few others.
- Readers of *Humor That Works* who offer ideas and anecdotes of their own, including: Angela, Noreen, Mary Kay, Tony, Jamie, Bradley, Palmo, David, Monica, and Joel.
- Websites where I find humor inspiration and funny videos, pictures, and text that keep me laughing (and sometimes from working), including: reddit.com, cracked.com, fark.com, theonion.com, thedailyshow.com, colbertnation.com, and a number of others.
- And finally: friends, family members, teachers, coaches, and audiences who have helped shape this sense of humor of mine.

INDEX[1]

1 The number shown is the way #.

Made in the USA
San Bernardino, CA
15 November 2016